The Stanislavsky Secret

Not a system, not a method but a way of thinking

Irina and Igor Levin

MERIWETHER PUBLISHING LTD.
Colorado Springs, Colorado

Meriwether Publishing Ltd., Publisher
PO Box 7710
Colorado Springs, CO 80933-7710

Editor: Arthur L. Zapel
Editorial coordinator: Renée Congdon
Cover design: Janice Melvin

Publisher's Cataloging-in-Publication
(Provided by Quality Books, Inc.)

Levin, Irina.
    The Stanislavsky secret : not a system, not a method but a way of thinking / Irina and Igor Levin. -- 1st ed.

    p. cm.
    Includes bibliographical references and index.
    1-56608-079-7

    1. Method (Acting) 2. Theater--Production and direction. I. Levin, Igor. II. Title.

PN2062.L48 2002   792'.028
                           QBI33-343

Contents

Introduction

The name Stanislavsky is known to millions of theatre-lovers across the globe. Yet few in the English-speaking world have an accurate understanding of what he actually taught in the last few years of his life when he pulled all his ideas together. This is not due to any lack of interest or want of serious study but to the circumstances in which his ideas traveled to the West.

It is a complex problem, but two main causes are evident. First, most actors, directors and students are dependent on translations which originally were heavily edited and cut and which have never been revised despite the wealth of material that has become available in the last half-century. They are, in the opinion of experts and scholars, not merely inadequate but, at times, misleading. However, no alternatives are available. Second, Stanislavsky never wrote down his final formulation of the "system" and the Method of Physical Action. He was in his seventies and extremely ill. Time was running out and in a final effort to pass on his ideas, Stanislavsky gathered round him a small group of students, handpicked assistants and colleagues from the Moscow Art Theatre, and created the Opera-Dramatic Studio at which, in the last three years of his life from 1936 to 1938, he put them through an intensive course of training in acting technique, play-analysis and rehearsal method. He thereby created a living tradition which has been handed down, generation by generation, from master to student, notably at the Moscow Art Theatre Studio Theatre School and the State Institutes of Theatre Art in Moscow and Leningrad (now St. Petersburg) until the present time. Igor and Irina Levin are among the inheritors of that tradition.

The great virtue of the "system" is its openness. That, indeed, is why Stanislavsky increasingly put the word in quotes. Basic principles aside, the "system" can and must be developed. In the years after the Second World War, when the Method of Physical Action had finally been accepted, many leading Soviet directors adapted the "system" to fit changing needs and changing circumstances, thus guaranteeing its creative power and preventing it from declining into a sterile set of rules, something which Stanislavsky feared and fought against all his life. The "system" had to live and grow. It was a way of creating living art, not a theoretical straitjacket.

Stanislavsky was also clear that the "system" had to be adapted to the needs of different cultures and traditions. It must not be mechanically transplanted across national boundaries. During the Moscow Art Theatre tour to the United States in 1923 and 1924, he realized how different American attitudes were from Russian. He developed a great admiration for the American people, their openness, their energy and their curiosity. The "system," he came increasingly to understand, could not be formulated and applied in the same way in New York as in Moscow. When he met the young Joshua Logan in the late 1920s, he told him firmly, "Don't copy me. Find your own answers."

Igor and Irina Levin summarize half a century of developments of the "system" in terms that are accessible to American artists and scholars. By concentrating on certain fundamental ideas, they cut through the many confusions that have arisen and present the Method of Physical Action in all its clarity, simplicity and logic. This they do, not through abstract theory, but through a series of contrasting, concrete examples, enabling the reader to see basic principles in action.

In addition, they remove any illusion that the Stanislavsky "system" can be identified with the Method as taught by Lee Strasberg at the Actors' Studio — an error, which, to be fair, Strasberg himself never committed. Here we are concerned with action, communication, interaction and conflict, not with a search for emotion which often has more to do with the actor himself than with the character he is playing.

This book may, and should, surprise many by its challenge to accepted notions, but its conclusions should be taken seriously.

Jean Benedetti
Stanislavky scholar and biographer,
author of Stanislavski and the Actor

Preface

The well-known Russian actor and director Konstantin Stanislavsky was the first to search for a practical method which would create a favorable environment for the inception of artistic inspiration during the performance of a role. He proposed that things which appear spontaneously and naturally in real life be recreated on the stage by means of a specially designed technique. This technique became known as "the Stanislavsky system."

The system created by Stanislavsky differs radically from all other previously existing theatrical systems in that from the very beginning it was directed towards the study of the internal psychological side of the creative process and not the external stage technique of the actor.

The Stanislavsky system went through a long period of development. Stanislavsky subdivided his system into two parts: "The actor's work on himself" and "The actor's work on the role." The first part, "The actor's work on himself," was described by him in two volumes, which were published shortly after his death in 1938.

The second part of Stanislavsky's system deals with the creative process of working on the play and the role. This part of his system was never finished, mainly because Stanislavsky continued his creative search until the very end, continually expanding, improving and changing the methods of work on the play. He discovered such a method only at the very end of his life.

He came to the conclusion that actions always appear as a result of confrontations or conflicts between characters. Consequently, the action is always directed at the partner in order to subordinate him, subdue his will, and thereby change his thinking in a desirable way. Thus, the action cannot exist without communion outside of the process of life interaction on the stage.

The development of the system did not cease with the death of its creator — his ideas were taken up, developed and introduced into theatre practice by his colleagues and followers. Nevertheless, the crowning point of the Stanislavsky system — the methodology of working on a role, based on a discovery made by Stanislavsky in the last two to three years of his life — still remains little known.

There are two reasons for this. First, Stanislavsky's experience is not condensed in his published volumes. He never described his later findings, and they are known only as recounted by his contemporary associates. One cannot understand the true essence of Stanislavsky's ideas or master his methodology by studying *An Actor Prepares* and *Building a Character*, or the draft versions of his unfinished *Creating a Role*. And the fact remains that Stanislavsky's books, not to mention their English translations, do not present a sufficiently clear picture of his ideas and methods. Stanislavsky's books only reflect the history of his creative search and not the final result at which he arrived at the end of his life.

The second reason is that during the political campaign unleashed in the Soviet press in 1950–51, Stanislavsky's latest discovery was condemned as ideologically unsound and, thereby, harmful to the Soviet theatre. As a result, during the following forty years, almost nothing was published on the theory and practical applications of this method.

One can truly understand Stanislavsky's legacy only by studying his ideas in their development and their movement through time, leaning not only upon his own books, but also on the books written by his closest colleagues and followers — Mikhail Kedrov, Vasilii Toporkov and Georgii Tovstonogov, who in the fifty years that followed, developed, expanded and tested Stanislavsky's ideas in practice.

* * *

This book is intended to be a manual for actors, directors and theatre students. Material from this book can be adopted for college-level courses in acting and directing.

The book consists of six chapters. Chapter One contains an historical review of the basic stages in the development of Stanislavsky's methodology of working on a play and a role. Particular attention is given to the post-Stanislavsky period of its development. The chapter contains numerous excerpts from Russian sources.

Chapter Two introduces the concept of the stage action. The meaning of the stage action is explained with a number of examples taken from real life and literature.

Chapter Three deals with the technique of performing stage action. Our attention is focused mainly on the element of actor's technique, *energy*, which is not sufficiently presented in the acting manuals. Our explanation of this element is illustrated in the example of a short story by Graham Greene and is followed by a set of exercises. We also touch upon the elements *emotional memory*, *object*, and *entering the stage*.

In Chapters Two and Three, we use examples of improvisations to show how to find and perform the stage actions. After that initial preparation, the reader will be ready to work on scenes from plays. In Chapter Four, the main stages of this type of work — the analysis of the given circumstances, conflicts and actions — are shown in the example of a scene from the comedy *Even a Wise Man Stumbles* by Alexander Ostrovsky. We also discuss the principle of dividing the play into a sequence of events, and we acquaint the reader with the fundamental concept of the Stanislavsky system — *the superobjective of the character*.

A specific technique of working on a monolog, based on revealing its inner contrasts and contradictions, is presented in Chapter Five. The technique is demonstrated in three monolog examples.

Chapter Six is devoted to the process of an actor's training. In a number of examples, we show how to create and perform improvisations that are intended to prepare the student for the work on a role, both psychologically and physically. We suggest also some exercises that can be performed individually, at home, without a partner.

In the Epilogue, we discuss *the actor's transformation* — the process of "merging" the actor with the character he portrays. The book also includes Notes and a Bibliography.

All translations of Russian texts, unless otherwise indicated, are our own.

Chapter One
The Development of the
Stanislavsky System, 1906-1990

For thirty-five years, I have been working on the laws of organic creativity.
Nobody in the world devoted or is devoting himself to this problem.
I establish the system and revise it again.
— K.S. Stanislavsky, April 1936

In 1906, the well-known Russian actor and director, Konstantin Stanislavsky (1863–1938), came to the conclusion that he had reached a critical point in his creative life. He realized that he had gradually lost the joy of stage creativity, that in the numerous replays of his roles he was gradually losing the live and sincere feelings which he had poured into his roles when he first created them, and that he was replacing the stale feelings with purely external, mechanical actors' techniques.

"In searching for a way out of the unbearable state of a person who is being forcibly exhibited and who is compelled against his human will and need to create, no matter what, an impression upon the spectators, we resort to false, artificial techniques of theatrical acting and we become used to them," Stanislavsky wrote in his book *My Life in Art*.[1]

Having become sharply aware of the harm and the erroneousness of an actor's being in such a state, Stanislavsky began to search for another emotional and physical state for the actor on the stage, which he called "the actor's creative state." Stanislavsky characterized the actor's creative state as "I am," which means "I am not simply on a stage, but I live, I feel, I think, and I behave in the same way as the character I am representing on the stage." Thus Stanislavsky believed that if only the actor were able to attain a true creative state, it would then suggest to him an expressive stage behavior, emotional response, pose, gesture, intonation, and facial expression.

He wrote:

> I knew then, that ... all artistic people, from geniuses to the simply talented, are capable to a greater or lesser degree of arriving at this creative state in mysterious intuitive ways; however, they are not empowered to regulate and to

control it arbitrarily.

I ask myself whether there are any technical ways of producing the actor's creative state? This does not mean, of course, that I wish to create inspiration itself by artificial means. Not inspiration itself, but simply a favorable environment for it, which I would like to learn to create within myself arbitrarily: that certain atmosphere, which causes inspiration to descend into our souls more frequently and readily.... How to go about making this state not appear unexpectedly, but be created by the actor's own will, on his "order"? And if it should be impossible to acquire this state immediately, could it be done piecemeal— put together, so to speak, from separate elements?[2]

Stanislavsky dedicated the following years of his life almost entirely to finding the answers to these questions. The result of his work was the creation of a theory of acting craftsmanship, which became known as "the Stanislavsky system." This theory did not remain immutable. It was constantly perfected and transformed in direct interaction with practice. For this reason, the system in its original form and Stanislavsky's final ideas, which he formulated not long before his death, may even appear to contradict each other when examined superficially.

The Initial Stage of the Development of the System

Stanislavsky pointed out from the very beginning that the sphere of subtle and imperceptible human emotions yields poorly to control and influence on the part of consciousness. Emotions cannot be fixed and summoned by an effort of the will. The emotions that have arisen within the actor involuntarily during the creative process cannot be reproduced voluntarily without the risk of violating nature.

The demand for emotionalism immediately draws the actor to a portrayal of feelings; that is, to some kind of general, abstract excitement. But as soon as he enters such a state, he enters the world of imitation, the world of external mimicry or cliché. For example, he begins to talk of love in a breathless, passionate whisper. One cannot play feelings; one cannot play the result.

For that reason, Stanislavsky immediately rejected emotion or feeling as the stimulus for the actor's creative state in the process of creating a character. He stressed the fact that one should search not for the feeling itself but for the given circumstances which produce the desired feeling. This principle — "the subconscious through the conscious, the spontaneous through the deliberate" — has remained in effect up to the present.

In the initial stage of the development of the system, Stanislavsky believed that the main thing was to understand how the character thinks. It seemed that the whole secret lay in appealing to the thought that was to produce the required emotions.

Accordingly, Stanislavsky introduced into the process of rehearsals a so-called period of work at the table, the purpose of which was to make all the facts and events of the play become intimate and clear to the actors. Knowledge of the life of the play is gained by proceeding from its external facts and events, which are the most accessible to one's consciousness, to a comprehension of the inner essence of the piece. It was presumed that this would help the actor find himself within the terms of the living role.

Having begun his work with the period of table rehearsals and a meticulous analysis of the characters and ideas of the future performance, Stanislavsky raised the general culture of the theatre and the actor. However, it soon became clear that to understand the role with one's mind did not necessarily mean to feel it. Therefore, Stanislavsky turned to a new stimulus of the actor's emotional nature — to his psychological state. At this stage of the development of the method, he proceeded on the assumption that both the behavior and the emotional reactions of the character are entirely stipulated by the psychology with which the playwright has endowed him. As the basic element, which determines the character's internal state, Stanislavsky introduces "desire," the volitional impulse. It is assumed that a successive performance of such "desires" within the circumstances of the play allows the actor to enter the psychological state of his character and thus arouse within himself feelings that are analogous to the emotions of the personage. In working with the role at this particular stage, the practice is to break the play up into small bits and search within each of them for volitional objectives that would answer the question: "What do I want?"

At the same time Stanislavsky introduces the concept of a "superobjective" — a more complex volitional objective, which must encompass all the separate, individual "desires" of the role. In Stanislavsky's opinion, to find the superobjective of a role generally means to understand the playwright's design of the entire role. Knowledge of the superobjective opens up to the actor the practical possibility of discovering the essence of the character's nature within the given circumstances of the play.

Stanislavsky remained at this stage of the development of the system for approximately twenty years. Throughout those years, numerous actors and directors became acquainted with his system and began to use it in their theatre practice. After the Russian Revolution and its aftermath, some of Stanislavsky's students and comrades found themselves outside of Russia, and they brought along to the West his ideas and his method of working on a role.[3]

The Beginning of the Method of Physical Actions (1929-1935)

However, toward the end of the 1920s, Stanislavsky himself began to gradually move away from the purely psychological approach to working on the role. He came to the conclusion that despite all its merits, such an approach continues to base itself on the shaky and almost imperceptible emotional side of creativity: that in order to truly desire something, one must not only grasp with one's mind, but also must feel deeply the object of one's attraction. Consequently, the necessary premise for all "desire" is still that very feeling which cannot be governed by our will.

Therefore, when working on a role, Stanislavsky suggested proceeding not from an internal or psychological state, but from the logic and the succession of physical actions performed by the actor. He came to the conclusion that only the actor's physical reaction, the chain of his physical actions on the stage, can summon the thought and the volitional impulse, and in the end, that very emotion for the sake of which the theatre exists.

It cannot be said, of course, that Stanislavsky deserves sole recognition for the concept of physical actions. Actors have always made use of these actions as a means of varying and ornamenting their acting by playing up different objects on the stage. Physical actions were regarded as a supplement, a sort of illustration to the actor's emotions. Only Stanislavsky, however, looked upon these actions not as a supplemental technique, but as a means of summoning within the actor the appropriate internal state. In 1929 Stanislavsky wrote:

> The objective is as follows: let the actor answer me with a clear conscience as to what he will be doing physically; that is, how he will act within the given circumstances, that have been created by the playwright, or the director, or the actor himself in his imagination. When these physical actions become clearly defined, it will only remain for the actor to physically perform them. Note that I am saying —

physically perform, and not emote, because with correct physical action, emotion will be born of its own accord.[4]

In 1935, Stanislavsky began to call his new approach to working on the role "the method of physical actions," often stressing, however, the conditional and imprecise nature of such terminology. He personally warned against interpreting "physical action" in its elementary sense, pointing out that it was not a matter of random movements, of those actor's adjustments which arise during the course of a performance, but of the psycho-physical actions in which the individual's entire being participates.

Stanislavsky always pointed out that every action contains both a psychological (internal) and a physical (external) side. If an action is not simply mechanical, it surely has a motive which induces it: It is impossible to think of the question "What am I doing?" without bringing up the parallel question "Why am I doing it?" Nevertheless, Stanislavsky rejected the term "psychophysical action," which he was often advised to use, because he feared that stressing the psychological side of action could lead to the actor's starting to act out feelings, mental states.

Stanislavsky recommended not approaching the study of a role speculatively or aloofly, but placing the actor right from the start into the position of an acting character, an active participant in all the events. The actor is faced with the question of what he would do, right here and now, if he were to find himself within the circumstances of the play, in the role of an acting character, and he is urged to answer the question not with a verbal discourse on the matter, but with real action. At the same time, Stanislavsky particularly stressed the fact that for him the main thing is not the physical action itself, but the justification of this action by the given circumstances.

This technique of working on a role is based on dividing the text of the play into bits, with each bit having a specific physical action. In the course of rehearsals the actor must work out, strengthen and fixate the line of physical actions of the role.

An analysis of a play by physical actions was demonstrated by Stanislavsky using as an example the third scene of Act III of Shakespeare's *Othello*. Stanislavsky wrote:

> The performer must not forget that Othello has yesterday become Desdemona's husband. All his yearnings are now towards her. Today he must engage in business affairs, but all the while all his thoughts are, of course, only

of Desdemona.[5]

With what must the actor live in this scene? Here is the line of purely physical actions: 1) try to find Desdemona as quickly as possible and embrace her; 2) she plays and flirts with Othello, so let the actor also play with her, let him make up a sweet little game; 3) Othello meets Iago on the way and, being in a good mood, plays with him, too; 4) Desdemona comes back to drag Othello to the ottoman and he again follows her playfully.[6]

Stanislavsky continued:

From the very beginning of the performance the role must be set up in such a way, that the actions determined by the physical line within the given circumstances may be clearly and easily performed. The actor must go onstage with the task of performing the actions truthfully and clearly — and nothing else ...

If, for some reason, today it is hard to believe in the action as a whole, at least believe in a part of it. For example: let us assume that in the scene that we were examining, the actor does not entirely believe in his merry state as a newlywed. So be it! — believe in at least part of it. Can you give an ardent kiss to the performer of Desdemona? Just physically give an ardent kiss? At the same time remember just for a moment and ask yourself: how would I kiss her if I were a newlywed? And nothing more for the time being. Go on immediately to the next action.

There is Iago standing and looking through a crack in the door. How should I give him a playful fright today? Perhaps I should make up some kind of prank? It is not at all important whether the prank is clever or not, whether it succeeds or not. Only one thing is important — to believe in this small physical action. And, at the same time, to remember for a moment: today I am a newlywed! And nothing more. Go on to the next action ...

This physical scheme of the role can be played in exactly five minutes: I come in, I give a kiss (I believe in it or at least partially), I joke with Iago (my belief grows), ... Desdemona pulls me, I play with her (I believe completely), etc. ...

If you follow the physical actions within the given circumstances, that is, in other words, you follow the scheme and believe in it; you can be assured that you are playing correctly.[7]

Thus, Stanislavsky assumed that, when an actor truthfully performs a sequence of physical actions, which naturally and logically follows from the character's given circumstances, it brings him into a psychological state, similar to that of the character he portrays, and, thereby, stimulates the truthfulness of his emotional reactions.

Stanislavsky sporadically used this approach to working on a role during rehearsals of individual scenes for his 1932 to early 1935 stage productions. However, already towards the end of this period his views underwent a considerable transformation.

Stanislavsky's Latest Discovery (1935-1938)

In the last years of his life, the seriously ill Stanislavsky almost completely withdrew from his work in the theatre. He spent all the time that his health permitted in working with the students of his theatrical studio, testing and perfecting in practice a new approach to creating the performance and the role, which he called his discovery, his new method.

Stanislavsky attached great importance to the process of communion during the performance of action:

> As you stand on the stage at the moment of creativity, performing the physical action and adapting to your object in the play, think only of how to express what you want to say as vividly, as faithfully, as imaginatively as possible. Firmly resolve to make your partner think and feel exactly as you do, make him see what you are saying through your eyes, hear through your ears.[8]

Thus, action is inseparable from the process of communion between partners. However, what lies at the base of the process of communion? What is the point of it? Stanislavsky replied that the point is that "each character has the utmost belief in his own rightness, and has the greatest and most ardent desire to immediately convert the other person to his own belief."[9]

At this point Stanislavsky took an extremely important step on the way to further development of his method: He determined the nature of the communion as an interaction between partners in the process of a struggle on the stage. This means that the actor performs his action in order to elicit from his partner some concrete real behavior, which he needs to attain his own concrete real goal.

Action becomes the instrument of practical influence over the partner, provoking a lively reaction.

Proceeding from there, Stanislavsky came to the conclusion that speech, words, also represent a variation of physical action, which he called verbal action: "The words of a role, on a par with its stage action, must be continuously active. The artist on the stage must be able to act not only with his hands and feet, but also with his tongue; that is, with words, speech, intonation." [10] He goes on to say: "The word and speech must also act; that is, they must force the other person to understand, see and think just like the speaker does." [11] Later Stanislavsky points out directly that "the transmission of one's thought is the same as action" [12] and ceases to distinguish between "physical" and "verbal" actions.

Simultaneously Stanislavsky answered the crucial questions: What constitutes the essence of the action, what kind of physical actions better awakes the actor's intuition and emotions? He pointed out that the action is always directed at the partner in order to subordinate him, subdue his will, and thereby change his thinking in the desirable way. It means that the action always appears as a result of confrontations or conflicts between characters and cannot exist without communion outside the process of life interaction on the stage.

All the elements of the actor's creative state, which were discovered and studied by Stanislavsky, are now united by him around a single concept — the action, which cannot be performed without the participation of creative attention, emotional memory, imagination, logic, the feeling of truth and belief, and must be embodied in word, movement, and the mise-en-scène. The performance of the stage action completely subordinates the actor's entire creativity, from his first to his last step on the stage. As a result, Stanislavsky essentially rebuilt the entire process of the actor's training. He pointed out that all the elements of the acting technique must not be worked out by themselves, but only in the process of performing the action. Otherwise, this may bring harm instead of benefit.

Stanislavsky never described his later findings, and they are known only as recounted by his associates of those years. "No one knows of what Stanislavsky spoke in the last years of his life," a close associate and pupil of Stanislavsky, Mikhail N. Kedrov (1893–1972) used to say. "Or, perhaps, only those few, who worked with Stanislavsky on *Tartuffe* or with me in *The Fruits of Enlightenment* [by Leo Tolstoy] and *The Winter's Tale*. But even those who went through these performances hardly absorbed all of it."[13]

At the end of 1937, the terminally ill Stanislavsky gathered a group of actors for a production of *Tartuffe*. The aim of the production was to run a practice test of his ultimate and newest ideas of working on a role. Stanislavsky appointed Mikhail Kedrov, whom he viewed as his successor, as director of the production and performer of the principal role.

Before the work began, Stanislavsky warned the actors that they should not think about the performance:

> I am definitely not planning to produce a play; a director's laurels do not interest me now. As I am leaving this life, I want to pass on to you the basics of this art. It is impossible to pass them on either in words, or in writing. They must be learned in practical application. If we achieve good results and you will gain understanding of this technique, you will propagate it and certainly develop it further.[14]

Stanislavsky only managed to go through eighteen rehearsals with the actors. The last rehearsal took place on April 27, 1938; the company was going away on a tour. On August 8, 1938, Stanislavsky was no more. The production was finished by Kedrov and put on stage in 1939.

The New Method Is Introduced into Theatre Practice (1939-1950)

Kedrov was of great service not only in that he carefully preserved Stanislavsky's final discovery and passed it on to subsequent generations of actors, but he also continued the search that was begun by Stanislavsky. He developed, added to, systematized, and tested in practice the ideas that were only outlined by Stanislavsky in general terms, concerning new ways of working out plays and roles. No one before him worked according to the method of physical actions,[15] not even Stanislavsky himself; the testing of this method was conducted in the form of individual exercises. With his productions, Kedrov proved that the method of physical actions is a living, contemporary method, a powerful instrument in the hands of the actor and the director.

Kedrov pointed out that if the director correctly follows the method of physical actions, he must first of all build up "a logic of behavior, a logic of action." However, "the logic of action cannot be fabricated, it must be found within the play itself, and one cannot substitute for it one's own subjective conjectures, which have no direct connection to the author's idea and often go against it."[16] "The method of physical actions is inapplicable to ideas that are perceived in a speculative manner, and shies away from them."[17]

Practical work on a play began with the play being divided into components. Within each component a certain event or occurrence takes place, which further develops the plot of the play. While working with the actors on the production of a play, Kedrov used to say:

> If we have determined the event, it is important to find the common factor which binds all of us together as a whole. This common factor in an event is its conflict — the moment of an active struggle between all the participants in the given event. It is absolutely imperative to find the state of conflict between the characters who are engaged in the event. Ask yourself: who is struggling against whom? What is the point of this struggle?[18]

> It is impossible to find the action if one does not understand the meaning of the event: what each of the participants is trying to achieve and what relations does he have with whom.[19]

Having worked out the scene–event and the conflict situation at the table, and having determined the action schematically, the actors then immediately went onstage and tried to recreate the essence of the struggle that was taking place. "It is important to me," Kedrov used to say to the actors, "that you watch all the time how you are influencing your partner, how you are modifying him, how you are forcing him to act differently."[20]

The actors who worked with Kedrov remarked on the novelty of such an approach to working out a role:

> Formerly, during a rehearsal, the actor would sit with a role and would mentally act out the role to himself from the notebook. He would thus be concentrated upon himself, he would be entirely withdrawn within himself, he would be afraid of splashing out the gleams of emotion that have appeared. He would constantly listen to himself, and test himself, and barely mutter the text of the role. He would not even need a partner.

> We did not have that situation. We proceeded on the assumption that each character is bound to his surroundings, to other people. He cannot be isolated from his partners. Everyone exerts influence over him and he

reacts to everyone's actions.[21]

While analyzing the play by events and mastering the logic of the character's actions, the actor involuntarily penetrates the latter's inner world. As a result, wrote Kedrov, "we deduce the internal motives, viewpoints, psychology, emotionality of the people shown in the play, and we arrive at an understanding of the ideas of the play itself and of each individual personage ... The action now becomes an expression of the very essence of the character."[22]

However, not everyone, including those in the Moscow Art Theatre, was ready to accept the new method as the final and absolute word in the Stanislavsky system. This was largely due to the fact that many of the actors and directors in the Moscow Art Theatre did not see any necessity in renouncing the customary, well-developed techniques of working out a role, which were based on the use of "volitional" objectives.

Despite all that, Kedrov succeeded in staging a series of performances at the Moscow Art Theatre, produced entirely according to the new method. These included Tolstoy's *The Fruits of Enlightenment* (1951) and Gogol's *The Inspector-General* (1966), which were great successes and remained in the theatre repertory for many years.

Due to the directorial and pedagogical work of Stanislavsky's immediate pupils Kedrov and Toporkov, the new method gained renown among theatricals and art critics by the late 1940s. This was largely due to the practical seminars which Kedrov conducted for a number of years among the actors of Moscow's theatres, and also to the publication of Toporkov's book, *Stanislavsky in Rehearsal*. A first attempt at interpreting the new method was also made at this time: this was a book by L. A. Okhitovich, *The Method of Physical Actions: a Monograph on the Final Discovery of K. S. Stanislavsky*, written at the behest of the Russian Theatrical Society.

The Political Campaign Against the New Method (1950-1951)

The propagation of the new method gave rise to bitter resistance on the part of Soviet theatrical bureaucracy. Not only was the new method not needed, it was actually harmful to the production of contemporary Soviet plays.

In the 1940s, Soviet drama degenerated completely into an instrument of political propaganda. Real people with real human interrelations and life-like conflicts disappeared from Soviet plays. The theatres were forced to stage colorless plays, all similar to one another, in which the only possible contradiction was an argument between "the good" and "the better." As a result, the inner world of the characters shown in these plays was proclaimed by the author through their words, rather than revealed through their mutual relations.

In 1950–51, a discussion devoted to Stanislavsky's creative legacy unfolded in the Soviet press. Soon this discussion turned into a campaign directed against the advocates of the method of physical actions. The struggle took place in the name of preserving the purity of the Stanislavsky system, which by that time had been declared the official doctrine of "advanced Soviet theatrical art."

The most furious attacks were directed against the method's underlying principle of a continuous struggle between the personages. Opponents of the method pointed out that this principle contradicts Soviet ideology, which asserted that "in Soviet society, where contradictions and conflicts between people assume a special, complex and delicate character, without being antagonistic as in bourgeois societies, the whole nature of the conflicts precludes a coarse scheme for the struggle."[23]

In joining the discussion, Kedrov noted that "all, literally all of the objections, criticism, and rejection of the method come from a misunderstanding of the starting points and fundamentals of the method."[24] He wrote:

> For the people who look ahead, it is very important to delve deeply into the legacy of Stanislavsky and to understand which part of it belongs to the past and which belongs to the future. We often grasp at what Stanislavsky had already rejected as an outdated stage, and rage at the new stage, in which he saw the living source for further development of the art.[25]

However, all attempts at discussing the new method in essence were in vain. The results of the "discussion" were soon summed up in an editorial in the newspaper *Soviet Art*, which said that "the advocates of 'the method of physical actions' have actually spoken out against the basic tenets of Marxist-Leninist aesthetics and psychology, having offered a new creative method which differs from and contradicts the method of social realism."[26] Stanislavsky's new method was officially finished, and the above-mentioned monograph of L. A. Okhitovich was never published.[27]

The 1950–51 campaign "in defense of Stanislavsky's legacy" had far-reaching consequences: During the following forty years, all publications dealing with the analysis and development of the new method disappeared almost completely, while those who actually used it in their theatrical work preferred not to mention it. The interpretation of "the Stanislavsky system" was taken over by a relatively small group of people, many of whom took part in the 1950–51 "discussion" against the new method.

In 1958, when the draft notes from Stanislavsky's archive pertaining to the initial period of the development of "the method of physical actions" were finally published,[28] they were immediately used to discredit the new method. The "interpreters of Stanislavsky" wrote: "The time has passed when Stanislavsky's ideas were transmitted by word of mouth. There is now an eight-volume publication of his works. Anyone who is interested in Stanislavsky's theoretical postulations has the opportunity of studying his authentic pronouncements."[29] The initial version of "the method of physical actions," from the period of 1929–35, was declared "Stanislavsky's ultimate discovery in the field of a new rehearsing technique, whose aim is to overcome the actor's passivity in the period when the play is being worked out at the table." This technique was called "the method of analysis by action."[30]

Post-Stanislavsky Development of the New Method

In May of 1938, a group of student graduates from the Department of Directing visited Stanislavsky's theatrical studio, where they watched a performance produced under the direction of Kedrov. After the show, Stanislavsky spoke with them and answered a volley of questions.[31] Eighteen years later, one of those students, Georgii A. Tovstonogov (1914–90), became the artistic director of the St. Petersburg Bolshoi Drama Theatre and soon turned it into one of the best known and most popular theatres in the Soviet Union.

During the following thirty-four years, Tovstonogov staged numerous Russian and Western plays. The distinguishing characteristic of Tovstonogov's productions was that he never had any flops. His shows could be liked or disliked, but they always aroused fiery debates and were always filled with deep meaning. His production of *The Idiot*, based on Dostoyevsky's novel, which the company played during its U.S. tour, achieved world renown.

The success of Tovstonogov's theatre was determined by two circumstances. First of all, in working on his plays, Tovstonogov used the version of "the method of physical actions" which was basically similar to the one described by Kedrov. (Tovstonogov himself, however, always referred to his method as a variant of "the method of analysis by action.") Secondly, Tovstonogov succeeded in bringing up in his theatre a group of actors who were able to work by this method.

In the literary legacy of Tovstonogov there are several writings (primarily from the 1980s), which give an idea of his method of working on a play. Generally, these are shorthand reports of his theatre rehearsals and separate notes on his seminars with young directors.

In working out a play, Tovstonogov proceeds on the assumption that

> every minute, every second of stage action represents an uninterrupted duel. Life on the stage does not exist outside of conflict. [Therefore,] our goal is to find a real struggle between two people within the circumstances given by the playwright, to bring them to this struggle.[32]
>
> The spectator places importance on the facet of the play represented by its conflicts, he watches for it. Conflict, action, event — this is what should interest us. If they are not built up, the actor will simply utter the memorized text; if they are built up, the words will be born of their own accord. Action is the ultimate expression of conflict in this very minute of the actor's life on the stage. The word is the final and not the initial result of the process.[33]

The director's objective is to find an exact "row of events" in the play itself, i.e., present the play in the form of a chain of successive events. In each event it is imperative "to discover the precise conflict which reveals the logic that is concealed in the author's text."[34]

The concept of a row of events, introduced by Tovstonogov, constituted an important step on the way to further development of the method which was begun by Stanislavsky and continued by Kedrov. However, although Kedrov's division of the play by events still took place on an intuitive basis, Tovstonogov already indicated a clear principle for such a division.

Tovstonogov particularly stressed the fact that the row of events exists in the play objectively: "One must not look upon the absence of a sharp plot as the absence of events. The director serves as the playwright's interpreter in the language of events and action."[35]

After going over the given circumstances, the mutual relations and the actions, the actors attempt to implement these actions onstage, elaborating and, if necessary, modifying them. Tovstonogov points out, that although the row of events must be clear to the director in advance, it can still undergo transformations and modifications in the course of the rehearsals, because "though having determined the essence of the conflict in the given portion of the play, the director cannot foresee how the actor will express it."[36]

"If the chain of events has been built up correctly," wrote Tovstonogov, "then the method guarantees the logic and the truth of the actor's behavior. This is the shortest path to the actor's logical and truthful existence on the stage."[37] As a result, "emotions may arise at the very first rehearsals. If one follows the action precisely, then emotions arise automatically, unconsciously."[38]

The methodology of analyzing a play, developed by Kedrov and Tovstonogov, was elaborated and systematized in our book, *Working on the Play and the Role*. It also contains an example of the practical application of the methodology to an entire play, Chekhov's *The Cherry Orchard*.

Chapter Two
Stage Action

The art of the theatre is the art of stage action. A work of drama becomes a theatrical work only from the moment when the literary characters, created by the playwright, find their embodiment in the actor's actions on the stage. Thus, the actor's action becomes the distinguishing characteristic of stage art in any of its forms. Take away action from the theatrical stage, and the theatre will disappear. Make the actor act on the stage, and the theatre will be reborn.

Many people erroneously believe that action is a collection of purely external manifestations. And the more movements you have on the stage, the more vividly and fully the character will be revealed.

Once we observed how during a rehearsal a director asked an actress playing the role of the maid to do something normally associated with the servant's duty — dusting, cleaning, sweeping the floor, removing dust-covers from furniture. He was not bothered by the fact that these "actions" were highly inappropriate during the scene where everybody impatiently awaits the arrival of the mistress of the house on an already overdue train. Not to mention that the house has been cleaned from top to bottom and the maid is dressed in her best outfit with her hair and face made up. Another director trying to "liven-up" the performance had asked an actress to be more mobile. "Do something with your hands," he said, "Doesn't matter what as long as there is more movement." Afraid of boring the audience, the director created a certain activity on the stage and called the activity action.

"Immobility of the one sitting on the stage does not define one's passivity," said Stanislavsky. "One may be motionless, but, nevertheless, be in genuine action. Often physical immobility is the direct result of an intense action."[1] Thus, a stage action is something other than movement, a physical activity.

According to Stanislavsky, stage action comes to life as the result of a clash between people. Stage actions cannot exist without disagreements, conflicts, or struggle. However, an overt display of the struggle may be absolutely unnecessary. People may smile, have conversations in low and soft voices, so that from the side, their confrontation would seem peaceful and idyllic.

Let us take a look at the following example of such a clash and the resulting stage actions.

Example 1: The Old Uncle

We imagine an old solitary uncle and his favorite nephew. We also imagine certain facts and occurrences, which we shall call "given circumstances," of the lives of these characters.

Now, it so happened that for a period of several years the nephew has been out of touch with the uncle who, in the past, has helped his nephew repeatedly during hard times. The conscience-stricken nephew finally finds enough time to visit the aging man. To please the old man he brings a bottle of first-rate champagne. However, the uncle displays no pleasure in regard to this visit and very coolly greets the nephew. Later the following dialog takes place:

> *(The nephew caringly sets his uncle down into an arm-chair and serves him a glass of champagne.)*

NEPHEW: *(Winking)* French!

UNCLE: *(Tasting)* This is not the real thing.

NEPHEW: Thirty dollars a bottle!

UNCLE: You definitely overpaid.

What has just happened? The text indicates a confrontation between two people where one tries to convince the other of something. What led them to this confrontation? A disagreement over the champagne? No, the reason lies much deeper.

Let us suppose that the nephew had brought, for example, a box of cigars or a sweater as a gift, instead of a bottle of champagne. The conversation would then have naturally revolved not around champagne, but around the cigars or the sweater; however, would the uncle have greeted the nephew more cordially, or would he have commended him for his gift? Of course not!

Conflicts between people arise out of not accepting some human qualities of one's opponent. Therefore a person, not some circumstance, object, or idea, is at the focal point of the conflict. So, the gist of the conflict in the given scene is not whether one character likes the champagne and the other one does not. The wine is just a pretext, which gives them an opportunity to express what they really think of each other. They speak about the champagne, but actually they declare who they are and how they perceive each other. And until their true relationship is revealed and the underlying reasons for the disagreement are discovered, it is impossible to understand what really happened in this scene and what the true meaning of the characters' words is.

But what could have caused the confrontation? His uncle's cool reception certainly makes the nephew feel uneasy. The nephew whose conscience is less than clear interprets such welcome as a sign that his uncle is angry with him. As a result, the nephew is compelled to confront his uncle in order to change his uncle's opinion. He tries to prove by his behavior that he's as attentive and caring as he has ever been, that he always remembers and thinks of his uncle, and even though he has not been able to visit him for a long period of time, nothing has changed between them. That is what we call the nephew's stage action (or action, to be short). Therefore, the action is a specific behavior, a certain tactic that the character uses to influence and subdue his opponent during a confrontation.

The other character, the uncle, also has a compelling circumstance which propels him into a struggle: His nephew has neglected him, has not thought of him for over three years, and now suddenly arrives as if nothing has happened, thinking that the slate can be wiped clean with a bottle of champagne. He is probably in need of his uncle's help again.

Correspondingly, the uncle purposefully does not make peace with his nephew and shows by his behavior that he will not be placated so easily. The aforementioned constitutes the uncle's stage action, but on the surface, it is manifested through dissatisfaction with the quality of the champagne.

The given example demonstrates that stage actions of characters are always hidden, concealed behind their words. The actions may be revealed and brought to the surface only by discovering the true relationship between the characters, or as we say, through discovering their conflict. But on the surface, there are only words — a conversation regarding the champagne.

The Characters' Conflict and Stage Actions

Now, let us define the necessary terminology and in a more concise formalized fashion, put down the conflict and stage actions of the characters.

As we have already demonstrated, confrontations among

people never arise out of thin air — they are always stipulated by the given circumstances. Among such circumstances, there is one which influences one of the sides to initiate the struggle. We shall call it the main circumstance, and the side that initiates and continues the struggle is the *leading* side (or leading character). Accordingly, the other, respondent side of the conflict shall be called the *led* side. In the given scene, the main circumstance is the fact that the nephew was coolly welcomed. Since such welcome motivated the nephew to initiate the struggle, he becomes the leading character and his uncle the led character of the conflict.

The relationship between the uncle and his nephew, their conflict, may be summarized in the following manner: The nephew considers himself a loving and devoted relative, having only the best and purest feelings for his uncle. However, the uncle sees his nephew as a selfish ingrate. This opinion is based upon the respective given circumstances: the nephew, for whom previously so much was done, has completely forsaken his uncle, disappeared, and has not been seen for the longest time. The nephew's action is to patch up their relationship, to get closer, to thaw, to pleasure the old man. He feels at fault. The uncle's action is to punish, to teach a lesson. He purposefully does not make up, clearly demonstrating that he is still upset.

It should be remembered that the stage action is always concrete and directed towards a partner. At the same time, it is very difficult to find an exact, faithful description of action, since words are not sufficient to embody the entire diversity of psychological shades of human behavior. Nevertheless, the search for an adequate definition of the action is extremely important, because when the actor begins choosing words that define one action or another, he is already creating. At this time one should not think of whether or not it is coming out in a literary fashion, but should write down the actions precisely and meticulously. Writing down the actions renders them concrete: In order to write down an action one must formulate it, because it is only possible to formulate that which one can imagine concretely.

Example 2: The Colonel

Everyday life is full of clashes between people. One only has to learn to see what people are trying to achieve through their words. For our second example, let us take a letter to the editor of *The London Times*:

> Recently I visited a city shirt maker in search of

detachable collars. The shop assistant received me indifferently while leaning on the counter reading a book. I drew myself up and said: "You sloppy man. You would never have made my regiment. Stand up and look at me while I am talking to you." He did!

Yours sincerely,

M. C. Shaw

Naval & Military Club

Let us analyze this scene in the same manner as the previous one:

1. Identify the leading character.
2. Find the circumstance that agitates the leading character and thereby prompts him to begin confrontation (the main given circumstance).
3. Determine the leading character's position in the conflict, an opinion, which he forms about either himself or his opponent.
4. Determine the behavioral tactic of the leading character — his action.
5. Find a given circumstance, which propels the led character into a struggle with the leading character.
6. Determine the led character's position in the conflict.
7. Determine the action of the led character.

Using our imaginations to fill in the gaps in the letter, we can see the described scene as follows:

M. C. Shaw, retired colonel, a man of years, honored and respected, walks into a shirt maker's shop. But a shop assistant, a young boy, ignores the colonel and pays him no attention. Such shabby treatment infuriates Mr. Shaw, and he is propelled into a struggle with the shop assistant, to change him, to modify his attitude and behavior. Accordingly, Mr. Shaw forces the young man to understand that he is dealing with someone who deserves and expects respect and consideration. This is his side in the conflict.

But how is he trying to accomplish this, what is his action? His action is to verbally thrash the shop assistant, to shake him up. The young man has forgotten himself and does not understand with whom he is dealing!

The client's behavior is the circumstance that determines the young man's position in the conflict: The client suddenly goes off the deep end, acting irrationally and speaking nonsense. Thus, to the shop assistant, he is a nut to keep away from. Naturally, the clerk's line of behavior, his action, consists of giving in by humoring Mr. Shaw. To pacify the client and to end the madness, he is ready to do everything that is asked — he even stands at attention.

Example 3: The Interview

Our friend from New York, Mrs. N, has told us the following true story:

Several years ago I had written a professional book, which subsequently was published by one of the houses. Eager to promote my ideas I had sent the book to one of the universities concurrently offering a program of seminars relating to the published subject matter. Not even a week had passed when I received a polite invitation for an interview from some Ms. X. When I arrived to be interviewed, I immediately recognized X, a lady whom I had previously met at a party and even had made pleasant small talk with. As it became apparent later, X also recognized me — she even remembered how I had my hair fixed up. To my greatest surprise, X received me less then amicably, coldly said that she was busy, and asked me to wait outside the office. Finally, after an hour of waiting, having lost all of my patience, I peeped into the office, and X motioned me to come in without offering any apologies for the lengthy wait.

In the office, there were two desks, with a secretary behind one of them, and farther, in the back, two armchairs separated by a small table. X left an armchair, where she was sitting during a lengthy conversation with one of the students, and sat down behind her desk. I was told to sit down in the armchair; the distance between us greatly hampered any possible conversation.

For the longest time, X did not allow me to get to the heart of the matter. At first, she interrupted me by an introduction to her secretary, and then began a long conversation with an instructor who happened to be passing by. Finally, after a short pause, X curtly said: "Speak!" I suggested to give a series of seminars on the subjects addressed by the book. "And what are you going to discuss?" asked X with an ironic smile on her lips. I succinctly described the contents of the book and asked whether X had the opportunity to take a look at it. X started to nod her head, said how "today was such a crazy day," and quickly added that she had to leave. She ended the interview by standing up from behind the desk and promising to consider my proposal and giving me a call shortly. Thus we parted. Needless to say that I have not heard anything from her since.

Let us analyze the preceding scene. Clearly, a conflict takes place, where Ms. X is the leading side — she dictates and sets the course of events. What propels X into a struggle with our friend? What is the main given circumstance? Of course, we may only guess as to her motivation, using facts available to us. One fact is that these two people had previously met. Therefore, we may guess that when X saw who came for an interview, she immediately realized that a mistake had been made: she accidentally invited a "wrong" person, a person who, for some personal reason, is not desirable. This is her position in the conflict.

Accordingly, X behaves in a very straightforward manner. She makes it obvious that our friend is not welcomed, and any kind of present or future cooperation is out of the question. Naturally, her action consists of keeping our friend at a distance, destroying the interview.

Now, let us consider the given circumstances of our friend, which are known to us through her own words. She was met coldly, forced to wait an hour outside the office, and never invited to come in. N interpreted such unfriendly behavior as a sign that somehow during their previous meeting X came to dislike her and is now doing everything in her power to get rid of N.

Having understood this, N does not allow her emotions to get the better of her: She stays. She decides that the interview must take place, so she walks straight into the office without invitation. Thus, N perceives herself to be above little petty personal vendettas, a professional who has come to discuss a matter of mutual interest. After all, why else would she have been invited for an interview? This is her position in the conflict. Accordingly, her tactic of behavior, her action, is to establish the contact with X, to rouse her interest.

Example 4: The Girlfriends

As a next example, we provide an improvisation of "The Girlfriends," evoked by old Hollywood films.

Two girls, who had lived in a small provincial town, had known each other since childhood and had dreamed together of becoming writers, followed very different fates. One became a popular writer, while the other happily married and devoted her life to family.

Sixteen years passed and the famous writer suddenly realizes that for a long time she has not created anything of any importance. She must leave the bustle of her life and find the spring of new creative themes and ideas. Rushing to change her surroundings, she arrives in the small quiet town of her childhood. Feeling overwhelmed by the memories, she decides to visit her schooldays girlfriend.

Her former close friend is stunned by the unexpected visit from such a famous personality. She ecstatically watches her famous friend, loudly compliments her on her looks and the way she is dressed, and, in confusion, does not know where to set her down, what to serve, or how to entertain her.

Her guest tiredly lowers herself down and pleasurably stretches on the couch. The lady of the house brings out an album in which she had been saving newspaper clippings about her famous friend for all these years. Her guest absentmindedly leafs through the album and with interest looks at the wall where the photographs of her hostess's husband and children hang. She changes the conversation to the subject of her friend's life and family. The housewife avoids what she supposes to be a boring topic and starts talking about her friend's latest book then runs out of the room to find it. When she returns with the book, her famous friend is already asleep on the couch.

We have described circumstances and characters' behavior. Now, let us determine the conflict between the two characters and find a short description of their stage actions.

Obviously, the active, the leading, side is the mistress of the house. What propels her into the struggle? What is the main given circumstance? Her main circumstance is that she is being visited by a famous person, her schooldays friend.

A modest housewife sees her guest as the pinnacle of success and popularity, a person belonging to a different, exciting, and overwhelming world. This is her position in the conflict. At the same time, her famous friend feels tired and emotionally exhausted. Her life seems to be empty and banal. She is full of doubts and disappointments and has lost all faith in her talent. In other words, she sees herself at a dead end. This is her side of the conflict.

It is easy to see that the hostess's action is to learn everything about the celebrity's life, while the writer's action consists of avoiding any conversation about herself or her life.

Example 5: The Jewels

The following improvisation is loosely based on *The Jewels*, a story by Guy de Maupassant.

> Monsieur Lantin, a clerk with a modest salary, met a girl at a party and married her. She was very poor, decent, and beautiful, and he was incredibly happy with her. She only had two faults: love of theatre and a passion for cheap fake jewelry. M. Lantin found it terribly tiring to go to the theatre after a day's work at the office. He begged his wife to go without him, and to please him she agreed. This love for the theatre soon aroused in her the desire to adorn her person. She began buying imitation jewelry, bringing home a new piece almost every evening.
>
> One evening while returning from the opera, Madam Lantin caught a cold and died a week later. Her husband was inconsolable. Very soon, the widower discovered that he lacked his wife's household sense and could not make ends meet. One day he completely ran out of money and decided to sell his wife's "trash." To his greatest astonishment, the jewelry turned out to be real, and he became a wealthy man.

For our improvisation, we are choosing one of the possible scenes out of the life of the happy couple. By no means do we have to use the scene described by the author, but the situation depicted in the story allows us to use our fantasy and imagine a scene, which could have been a part of the characters' lives.

Let us suppose the leading side in this scene is Mme. Lantin, and the main given circumstance is that today she has received a gift of a beautiful necklace with big diamonds.

As always, construction of the conflict has to start with the leading character's interpretation of the main given circumstance in a manner leading to the confrontation. In other words, the circumstance must be presented as it is seen through the eyes of the leading character in his own interpretation.

For example, Mme. Lantin sees herself as the luckiest woman in the world who has everything any woman can wish for — total freedom, a wonderful, convenient husband who adores her, and wealth.

Mme. Lantin's suggested behavior could be humming a waltz, spinning around the room, constantly fondling and putting up the necklace from one mirror to the next and adoring her reflection. Then with a happy smile on her lips, she flies over to her husband, wraps her arms around his neck, and drags him into a waltz.

The wild exhibition of his wife's happiness over the purchase of such cheap pieces of glass is the precise circumstance which forces M. Lantin into confrontation. He sees her as a naive child who lives in fantasy and is satisfied with trivia. This is his side of the conflict. Not willing to spoil her naive happiness, M. Lantin allows himself to participate in her festivities.

On the basis of the described behavior of our characters, the wife's action is "to pull into her festivities," while the husband's action is "to play along, to participate in her childish game."

The Focal Point of a Conflict

Any confrontation, by its very nature, assumes a point of discord over which an argument begins and develops. In our conflicts, that point is always one of the characters involved in the conflict. Correspondingly, the essence of the conflict is defined by the difference of opinions about this character.

Thus, only two types of relations are possible between the parties involved in a conflict. In one case, the leading character imposes his view of himself on his opponent. In the other case, the leading character states how he sees his opponent. In both cases the leading character strives to subordinate the other side to his will, and thereby force on that side his own point of view. The opponent resists and defends his position.

The above implies that a conflict without a common point of contention is meaningless: In such a case neither character has any cause for confrontation, since no one is challenging the other's opinion. Another requirement is the manifest presence of two confronting sides in a conflict. This means that conflicts cannot involve such abstract concepts as "conflict of conscience," "conflict with society," and the like, in which there is no physical opponent.

The considered examples illustrate both types of relationships between the participants in a conflict. In the scenes "The Interview" and "The Girlfriends," the leading character states how he sees his opponent; correspondingly, the led character is the focal point of the conflict. In the scenes "The Old Uncle," "The Colonel," and "The

Jewels," the leading character declares who he is which means that he is in the focus of the conflict.

Communion on the Stage

The nature of all relations on the stage may be characterized as interactions between partners in the process of a struggle. As we already know, this struggle consists of each partner imposing upon his opponent his own position in the conflict, using his stage action for this purpose.

While counteracting each other, the actors evaluate the extent of their opponent's resistance, watching how he performs his action — how he looks, how he moves, his intonation, etc. Proceeding from this evaluation, the actor decides how and with what intensity he can best respond to a look, to a word, how to react to a bodily movement; that is, how to perform his action most effectively and uphold his position in the conflict.

Therefore, the actor to whom speech is directed does not simply wait his turn to enter the conversation, but continuously evaluates the behavior and words of his partner, while engaging in a silent struggle with him. He influences him with his whole physical behavior and with his actual silence, which is often more eloquent than words.

The Actor's Adjustments

An actor can practically perform stage action by diverse means. Stanislavsky called all concrete external forms of performing stage action "the actor's adjustments."

The real-life scene that we had described earlier, "The Interview" provides a perfect example of such adjustments: Ms. X seated our friend at such distance that it made conversation between them difficult. Twice she interrupted the interview (first by introducing the secretary, then by stopping the teacher who was walking by), and finally she mentioned her busyness, broke off the interview, and left. These adjustments, which X discovered spontaneously, precisely expressed the essence of her action, which we defined as "wrecking the interview."

The correct arrangement of actors that is discovered during rehearsals is nailed down and becomes the mise-en-scène to be repeated at each performance. If, for instance, we were to stage "The Interview," we would use the mise-en-scène unintentionally created by X.

However, it is impossible to predict which adjustments the

actors will perform within the framework of the given mise-en-scène: Which bodily movements, facial expressions, intonations, etc. they would use. These actors' adjustments should never become fixed. "To repeat adjustments means to deaden the role and dry up the play," Stanislavsky used to say. "Your acting should always remain half-impromptu."[2]

Any attempt on the actor's part to copy previously discovered adjustments will lead him to a loss of stage action. An actor who concentrates his attention on observing the external form of action does not need a partner. Such an actor excludes himself, of necessity, from the process of an active struggle with his partners and from the process of stage interaction. The actor's playing becomes mechanical: He does not live here and now in the given circumstances of the play and does not actively participate in its conflicts.

Thus, the freshness and naturalness of the performance rests in its improvisation and in the manner in which the actor feels and adjusts to his partner on the spot; the way he feels his action today. No two performances are alike; a role is never played alike twice. Today's performance differs from yesterday's, while tomorrow's performance will differ from today's.

Action and Activity

The entire material of this book is concentrated on the stage action, which is always aimed at subduing the opponent in a conflict situation. However, some characters may be present on the stage and at the same time not be engaged in any conflict. Their conflicts may begin later, when the relevant given circumstances appear, or even may not begin at all. That does not mean that such characters remain inactive. Their stage existence is still conditioned by the given circumstances having been created by the playwright, or the actor himself.

As an example, let us consider a scene from Chekhov's *The Cherry Orchard*. In Act I, a maid, Dunyasha, appears on stage where two characters, Anya and Varya, are engaged in a conflict. Dunyasha does not participate in this conflict; she comes in to carry out a physical task that was ordered by her mistress — to make coffee. Therefore, speaking about her activity, we can't use the word "action," which has been reserved as a special term to refer to a behavior tactic aimed at influencing the opponent in a conflict.

Dunyasha begins her action only when the entrance of a new character, Yasha, originates their conflict. She still continues to brew coffee — it is her duty, but now this activity is not the end in itself. Making coffee becomes one of Dunyasha's adjustments, one of the outer manifestations of her action which is naturally directed at Yasha.

Let us explain what it means. In this scene, Dunyasha's action is to attract and captivate Yasha.[3] Correspondingly, she uses the process of making coffee to show off, in every way, her irresistible appearance and delicate manners that she is so proud of. Thus, Dunyasha's physical activity during her coffee making becomes the integral part of her action, which is aimed at arousing interest in her person. In other words, making coffee becomes one of her adjustments.

Chapter Three
Elements of Acting Technique

In the previous chapter we have shown that stage action represents a behavioral tactic, which the character uses in order to impose his point of view and influence his opponent. A direct consequence of this is that stage action cannot exist in the absence of confrontation, a struggle between the characters.

Conflicts between imaginary heroes of literary works do not differ, in principle, from conflicts in real life. In both cases, the conflicting sides attempt to suppress the opponent, using a certain chosen line of behavior. This, of course, is not surprising: When creating his work, the author cannot step outside the bounds of everyday human experience, cannot change or go around the typical characteristics of human psychology. No matter who the characters of a literary creation may be, creatures from outer space, fairy-tale animals, or incorporeal spirits, the author necessarily describes their mutual relations and behavior in an anthropomorphic manner.

At the same time there is a distinct difference in the way a struggle takes place in real life and on the stage. When people enter a struggle in real life, they can only surmise what their opponent's behavior will be like, and they never know precisely how the struggle will end. Therefore, confrontations between people are full of the unpredictable, the unexpected, which evinces involuntary and richly emotional reactions from them. Only a prophet can remain impassive in the process of a confrontation: In contrast to other people, he has prior knowledge of the end result.

To some extent, the actor comes through as such a prophet. In contrast to real life, the outcome of any struggle in the play is predetermined; its process is firmly fixed by the author and no longer conceals any surprises. Therefore, all real need for a struggle disappears, and because of this the actor is deprived of a natural basis for the arousal of truthful reactions and feelings. As a result, words often become the sole means of an actor's expressiveness: The actor begins to push words, to raise or lower his voice, to aspirate them, etc.

In order to "forget" the end result and to re-live everything from the beginning, the actor has to recreate the character's conflicts and actions. However, to perform the stage actions one needs a certain acting technique. The well-known Stanislavsky system is used by us as such a technique. To a limited degree, elements of this system are described in a number of textbooks on the acting technique. Therefore, we do not find it necessary to examine the majority of such elements in our book. Our attention will be focused mainly on the exceedingly important and inadequately represented element in the current literature of the acting technique: *energy*. We will also briefly touch upon the elements *attitude to the object* and *emotional memory*.

Energy

Every stage action is performed with a certain degree of intensity or, as we will say, with a certain energy. This external manifestation of activity, which includes the actor's facial expressions, speech and movement, should be preceded by an internal, imagined movement, which must be created within the actor's body.

Stanislavsky said that only through an internal feeling of movement can the actor understand and feel the character: how his hero moves, talks, performs his stage action. One must practice a lot in order to become used to the feeling of the flow of movement through the muscular system or the flow of motive energy through one's body.

"Let us suppose for a moment that all your energy is concentrated, so to speak, in your heart, that it is like a ball of mercury," said Stanislavsky. "Now I have rolled it over into my shoulder. Now all my energy is in the shoulder. Then onward into the elbow! Into the wrist! Into the hand! Along the fingers! Backwards! Into the feet, into each toe, etc. This peculiar form of exercise will train the student to the point whereby we are actually able, by means of an extended index finger (the 'mercury' is at the tip of the nail at this moment) to force others to go wherever we want them."[2] Thus, the energy can be moved not only within us, but also be sent beyond the bounds of our body, being directed towards partners and objects.

The world-famous actor, director, and drama teacher Michael Chekhov proposed a similar system of exercises, whose purpose is to develop within oneself the sensation of the flowing energy.[3] As one such exercise he suggests imagining that within you, let's say in your chest, there exists a center from which flow the actual impulses for all your movements. This center is imagined to be seen as a source of all inner activity within your body. Before making any movement, you must first direct the necessary flow of energy from within this center, following an instant later with the actual movement so that the power flowing from your body leads you and precedes the movement itself. This dispatch of energy should not be terminated immediately upon the execution of the movement, but should continue to "radiate" outside the body for a bit longer. Concurrently, there may be any number of combinations of power and tempo for this energy. For example, one can send a weak flow of energy in either quick or slow tempo, or a powerful flow in moderate or forceful tempo.

It is recommended to repeat this exercise further, moving the imaginary center of energy to different parts of the body. For instance, you can imagine that the center of energy is located at your fingertips, or between your eyebrows, or at the end of your nose, etc. As a result you develop the feeling of internal power flowing through and out of your body.

However, to produce within yourself the feeling of flowing energy is not yet enough for the performance of stage action: It is important to also understand how to direct this energy at your partner. As an example, let us consider the scene "The Old Uncle." The nephew, seeing that his uncle is cold towards him, directs a continuous flow of energy at him. The nephew becomes more and more attentive and sympathetic. The uncle, engrossed with his nephew's solicitous behavior, conceals his joy at the nephew's arrival. He continuously curbs and restrains the energy bursting inside of him. Although his energy continues to burst forth toward his partner, he restrains it, hides it. We can well imagine that the more attentive and sympathetic the nephew will be, the more the uncle will continue to thaw. He almost has no power left to restrain the energy which is ready to pour out onto the nephew whom he loves and is ready to forgive. Now the energy has broken out a bit, and it costs the uncle a great deal of effort to keep it at least minimal in this state.

Thus, when performing the nephew's action (to mend relations, to draw nearer, to win over), all of the actor's energy freely pours out onto the uncle. In the case of the uncle, however, when performing his action (to punish, to teach a lesson), the actor must intentionally restrain, take away his energy from his partner. This particular technique of dispatching a flow of energy toward one's partner we will call a dispatch of energy with impediment.

Another version of the dispatch of energy with impediment can be seen in the example of "The Girlfriends." One can picture the leading character in this scene, the mistress of the house, pouring out an unrestrained and unimpeded flow of energy onto her guest: She avidly wants to learn everything about the celebrity's life. But the action of the other character, the writer, consists of avoiding conversation about herself. Therefore, everything within her resists talking about her life. However, she has come here as a guest and must keep the conversation going somehow. The writer is compelled to produce energy within herself and force it to flow at her partner: Her energy disperses, slips away, as she makes an effort to push it at her partner, reluctantly answering the hostess's questions. Thus here, as in the case of the uncle, the energy overcomes impediments. However, where the uncle restrains energy that is bursting forth from him, the writer produces energy and directs it with much effort toward her partner.

The dispatch of energy with impediment reflects an internal struggle that takes place within a person. It is important for the actor not to miss such moments, since they will lead to an enrichment of the character he is trying to create. For example, if in the above-mentioned examples the energy were to flow onto the partners without impediment, we would miss the impression of the uncle being offended or the writer being anxious.

Thus, the flow of energy may be directed towards the partner either freely or with impediment. Concurrently, the flow of energy that is directed with impediment can be of two types: 1. Energy that bursts forth towards the partner and must be restrained by the actor, and 2. Energy that must be produced by the actor and pushed onto the partner.

The exploration of the type of energy to be dispatched is a psychophysical process. Following the logic of the given circumstances, conflict and action, at first the actor sees his character in his mind's eye, feels the pulse of his life, estimates which direction of the flow of energy is the most "natural" for his stage action. In other words, at first the actor tries to play in his imagination the movement of energy. Such a search for an adequate movement of energy leads the actor to a perception or a presentiment of future action. Then the perceived type of energy movement may be fixed by the actor and repeated from performance to performance.

At the same time, it is impossible to foresee in advance how the actor will produce the variations or, as we say, the distribution of the energy according to intensity and tempo at each performance. This depends on how he will evaluate his partner's resistance, how he will react to it. In other words, how the interaction will take place on stage.

For instance, let us suppose that today the actor playing the role of the uncle ("The Old Uncle") is too resistant. Evaluating the situation, the nephew will be forced to send a more powerful flow of energy in order to sweeten him up. In another performance, the uncle may be less resistant, somewhat more tractable, and the nephew's pressure will adjust accordingly. Concurrently, while varying the force and tempo of their energy, the actors retain the previously chosen direction of energy: The nephew's flow of energy remains unrestrained, while the uncle's remains constrained.

Thus the type of energy dispatch towards the partner is predetermined by the given conflict and action, while the distribution of energy according to force and tempo is always unconscious, improvised.

Now we will continue our analysis of this important element of the acting technique using an excerpt taken from the short story *A Shocking Accident*, by Graham Greene. This literary material provides a vivid example of the dispatch of energy with impediment and how the characters control it.

Example: *A Shocking Accident* by Graham Greene

Jerome was called into his housemaster's room in the break between the second and the third class on a Thursday morning. He had no fear of trouble, for he was a warden — the name that the proprietor and headmaster of a rather expensive preparatory school had chosen to give to approved, reliable boys in the lower forms (from a warden one became a guardian and finally before leaving, it was hoped for Marlborough or Rugby, a crusader). The headmaster, Mr. Wordsworth, sat behind his desk with an appearance of perplexity and apprehension. Jerome had the odd impression when he entered that he was a cause of Mr. Wordsworth's fear.

"Sit down, Jerome," Mr. Wordsworth said. "All going well with the trigonometry?"

"Yes, sir."

"I've had a telephone call, Jerome. From your aunt. I'm

afraid I have bad news for you."

"Yes, sir?"

"Your father has had an accident."

"Oh."

Mr. Wordsworth looked at him with some surprise. "A serious accident."

"Yes, sir?"

Jerome worshipped his father: The verb is exact. As man recreates God, so Jerome recreated his father, from restless, widowed author into a mysterious adventurer who traveled in far places like Nice, Beirut, Majorca, even the Canaries. The time had arrived, about his eighth birthday, when Jerome believed that his father either "ran guns" or was a member of the British Secret Service. Now it occurred to him that his father might have been wounded in "a hail of machine-gun bullets."

Mr. Wordsworth played with the ruler on his desk. He seemed at a loss how to continue. He said, "You know your father was in Naples?"

"Yes, sir."

"Your aunt heard from the hospital today."

"Oh."

Mr. Wordsworth said with desperation, "It was a street accident."

"Yes, sir?" It seemed quite likely to Jerome that they would call it a street accident. The police of course had fired first; his father would not take human life except as a last resort.

"I'm afraid your father was very seriously hurt indeed."

"Oh."

"In fact, Jerome, he died yesterday. Quite without pain."

"Did they shoot him through the heart?"

"I beg you pardon. What did you say, Jerome?"

"Did they shoot him through the heart?"

"Nobody shot him, Jerome. A pig fell on him." An inexplicable convulsion took place in the nerves of Mr. Wordsworth face; it really looked for a moment as though he were going to laugh. He closed his eyes, composed his features and said as rapidly as possible, "Your father was walking along a street in Naples when a pig fell on him. A shocking accident. Apparently in the poorer quarters of Naples they keep pigs on their balconies. This one was on the fifth floor. It had grown too fat. The balcony broke. The pig fell on your father."

Mr. Wordsworth left his desk rapidly and went to the window, turning his back on Jerome. He shook a little with emotion.

Jerome said, "What happened to the pig?"

This was not callousness on the part of Jerome, as it was interpreted by Mr. Wordsworth to his colleagues (he even discussed with them whether, perhaps, Jerome was yet fitted to be a warden). Jerome was only attempting to visualize the strange scene to get the details right. Nor was Jerome a boy who cried; he was a boy who brooded, and it never occurred to him at his preparatory school that the circumstances of his father's death were comic — they were still part of the mystery of life.

Conflict and Actions

In this scene, the leading character is obviously the housemaster. His given circumstances: The father of one of the school's students, Jerome, has died in unusually comical circumstances — a pig fell from the balcony onto him and broke his neck. The housemaster has been tasked with the sad duty of informing the boy of what happened.

The housemaster imposes that Jerome is not alone, that he, the housemaster, takes part in Jerome's life and sincerely shares his misfortune. This is the housemaster's side in the conflict. Correspondingly, his action will be to prepare, to guide the eight-year-old boy to the correct comprehension of what has happened.

The housemaster is sure that the circumstances surrounding the accident are so ridiculous that at the mention of them everyone will succumb to involuntary laughter. He himself struggles to control himself and stay within the bounds of decorum.

So, how does he perform his action, that is, what are his adjustments? The housemaster's adjustments consist of avoiding a direct and candid talk, of omitting any details of the accident. Let us see how, according to the author's description, the housemaster performs his action. In order to avoid mentioning the comical details, the housemaster first recites that an accident has occurred, then calls it a street accident, and then simply mentions the fact of death. When the housemaster is finally forced to touch upon details, he mutters them quickly, calls the occurrence "a shocking accident" and, unable to contain his laughter, turns away to the window, thus cutting off the conversation. Jerome does not receive an answer to his last question.

Jerome's given circumstances: The housemaster is not at ease, he has greeted Jerome with fear and is obviously hiding something. As soon as the housemaster mentions the accident, it becomes obvious to Jerome that something terrible has happened to his father — the father was probably caught in crossfire. However, Jerome is ready for anything: He knows that his father leads a mysterious and dangerous life.

Jerome's action is to wait, to compel the housemaster to give him all the details of the "accident." By his curt replies, Jerome does not allow the housemaster to bring the conversation to an end and forces him to provide more and more details of the happening. Therefore, the pig is just a new, unexpected detail of his father's assassination. And, as the author said, the purpose of Jerome's last question was to get all the details right.

Distribution of Energy

The housemaster hides, restrains his energy just to avoid doing something unseemly. At the end of the scene, when he is forced to mention the ridiculous circumstances surrounding the death and he is overcome by a paroxysm of laughter, his energy refuses to stay in check, and it costs him a great deal of effort to prevent it from bursting out. A struggle then takes place: The energy tries to break loose, while he forces it back. This is the reason for his quick, bungled speech.

Jerome restrains his energy, not allowing it to burst out. He is in despair. He freezes with fear, but he has to keep his *sangfroid* and find out what exactly has happened with his father. To the housemaster this restraint appears as indifference or callousness.

Energy Exercises

The following exercises are aimed at the development of the feeling of the flow of energy in the various parts of your body. Every exercise will begin by imagining certain circumstances necessitating the flow of energy.

Exercise 1

You are trying to steal an apple from somebody else's orchard. It should be done silently, without a crunch of breaking twigs. What kind of energy flow will you send from your fingertips? You may, for instance, send a moderate flow of energy in a very quick tempo or a weak flow in a slow tempo. Everyone will do it differently: it depends on one's individuality and the additional circumstances imagined.

Let us change the circumstances. Now it is your own orchard, and you want to pluck an apple, which has ripened and is just about to fall. What flow of energy will you send in this case?

Exercise 2

You are on the beach. A horsefly sat on your right shoulder blade and is biting you. Send a flow of energy from the shoulder blade to drive the horsefly away. Don't stop the flow of energy immediately; continue to "radiate" it beyond the boundaries of your body.

Exercise 3

Today you put on a pair of beautiful new shoes and go to a party. Suddenly, one shoe is sucked into the mud. You want to shake the mud off, but you are afraid to get your stockings (trousers) dirty. What kind of energy should you send from the toe (through my leg) to do this movement?

Exercise 4

You're driving a car. The wind blows your hair into your eyes; you can't see the road. What flow of energy are you dispatching from your forehead to move the hairs?

Exercise 5

A beautiful butterfly sits on your shoulder. You are trying not to frighten it away. How will you dispatch the energy through your body? Now, instead of sending a flow of energy out of your body, you direct it inward. You hold back the energy in order not to move, not to frighten the butterfly. In other words, you are contracting the muscles of your body.

Exercise 6

It is an awfully cold and windy day. You are shrinking, trying to get warm. This again is an exercise of contraction. The energy flow is directed inward.

Exercise 7

You are tossing an imaginary ball into the air using various parts of the body: arms, feet, shoulders, elbows, knees. Again, do not interrupt the flow of energy from the corresponding part of your body, continue to "radiate" it beyond the bodily boundaries. Repeat the exercise adding new circumstances; for instance, you are on a tilted roof, on a tree branch, walking the tight rope in the circus.

Another type of dispatch of energy is one with impediment, as if a person is deciding or hesitates whether to do something or not. For instance: whether to jump into the cold water or not, open somebody else's letter or not, hail someone on the street or not, etc. The related exercises are created in this way: First, the student imagines some circumstances and invents an inner monolog, which expresses the process of hesitation. Then he performs the exercise directing the energy flow in conformity with the words of monolog, which may be spoken out loud or in his mind.

Exercise 8

Given circumstances: You're put on a diet. You're forbidden to have any sweets. However, there is a full container of ice cream in the refrigerator.

"Such an awful temptation! No, I am already through with sweets. But, why not start the diet tomorrow? What difference would a day make? None. I'll eat ice cream for the last time, and then I'll never do it again! But, this is no good, after all, I have decided to diet. I must start immediately. On the other hand, nothing would happen if I just have a little bite. I'll eat a tiny spoonful and throw the rest away. No, I can't. I have to prove to myself that I have the will power!"

I'm suppressing energy that pulls me to the refrigerator. I'm pushing the energy back, but it escapes, and I'm forced to suppress it again and again.

Exercise 9

Given circumstances: I am in an overcrowded subway car. Suddenly I notice a young man casting glances at an open bag hanging on a woman's shoulder. He looks like a pickpocket.

"Should I warn her, or is it better not to get involved? Yes, I should. But to reach her, I have to struggle through the crowd. It's rather awkward! The man is getting closer and closer. It looks as if he will push his hand in her bag at any minute, snatch the valet, and get out of the car. But maybe I'm wrong; maybe that's just my imagination? Maybe he has no such intention? Still, I have to warn her."

My energy is bubbling inside, bursting forth towards the woman. I make an energetic movement in her direction, but immediately pause, being overwhelmed by doubts. My energy slips away, diminishes; there is not enough energy to move me forward. However, I force myself to create energy, I have to warn the woman, and I push my way through the crowd.

Exercise 10

Given circumstances: I'm a very punctual person and very proud of it. Tonight at six o'clock I have an appointment with an influential man, and I need to make a good impression. However, I've arrived twenty minutes early. It just happened, I couldn't help it, and now I have to wait on the street. The weather is terrible; it is very cold, my hands and feet are freezing.

"Maybe I should not wait any longer and enter the house? No, it's a matter of principle! I cannot surrender, cannot be diminished so easily! I have to master myself!" Energy is raging inside of me, driving me into the warm house. I'm trying to suppress it, hold it back, but the energy is slipping away every time. At last, I cannot restrain it anymore, and I bang on the door.

Exercise 11

Given circumstances: I have a burden on my conscience. I've done a dishonest thing, and I regret it deeply. It's beyond my strength to hide it any longer, and I've written a letter with my confession. Now I'm going to put it into the mailbox. A severe punishment, possibly even prison, lies ahead.

"My life will be changed. Where can I find the courage to do that? Maybe I should not send the letter? But how can I go on living with such a burden! No, I have to do it, I have to overcome my fears and mail the letter!"

I'm producing energy to push the letter through the slot, but every time, my energy weakens and disperses. Again and again, I gather the energy, pump it up, and eventually mail the letter.

The Object

The object is a means of salvation for the actor: It helps him to concentrate, to create a mise-en-scène, to implement his stage action more precisely and vividly. At the same time one can often see how, in an attempt to create a certain physical activity on the stage, actors will grab at any chance object in order to mask the absence of stage action. When the actor does not know what he should do on the stage (i.e., he does not know his stage action), he always tries to find some object — for example, a cigarette, a glass, a handkerchief — anything in order to keep himself busy on the stage.

The objects which the actor uses in performing his stage action may be roughly subdivided into two groups.

a. Objects which bear a psychological load. These are objects with which the character has a certain relationship. Through this relationship one can understand who the character is, where he is, why and what he is doing, and for what purpose. Such objects help the actor immerse himself in his character's way of thinking, reveal the interrelations between the characters, see pictures of the character's imaginary life, and stimulate the emotional memory.

b. Objects which do not bear a psychological load and are simply used as tools, helping to perform the action. Successfully discovered tools make an actor's performance vivid and full of fantasy.

Let us now consider in which of the two categories do the objects belong that have been mentioned in our scenes.

In *A Shocking Accident*, the author mentions only one object, a ruler, which helps the housemaster to perform his action. By playing with the ruler, the housemaster avoids direct eye contact with Jerome and that helps him pull himself together.

It is obvious that for both characters in "The Old Uncle," the champagne bottle bears a psychological load. For the nephew this is not just any bottle that has randomly come into his hands, but is an object that has a definite biography, to which he has a definite relationship. For him this bottle is tied to images of how he searched for it meticulously and at length in the hopes of pleasing the old man and making amends. For the uncle this, too, is not just any bottle, but a costly present that testifies to the attention and love that his nephew bears him.

In "The Jewels," the necklace also bears a psychological load for both characters. For the wife the necklace leads to images of her secret life, of which her husband knows nothing. For the husband the fake necklace represents yet another testimony of his destitute and hopeless existence.

Now let us imagine that in "The Colonel," Mr. Shaw holds in his hand a cane, which he beats in time with his words. This object does not bear a psychological load: The character has no relation to it in this particular scene. Mr. Shaw uses this object as a tool, in order to perform his action more vividly.

In "The Girlfriends," the photographs of the hostess's husband and children, which hang on the wall, bear a psychological load and help the actress, who plays the role of the writer, believe in where she is, who she is, and what her relationship to the mistress of the house is. That is, the writer is in the home of her former girlfriend, who got married and raised two children during the years that they had not seen each other. Newspaper clippings and the famous girlfriend's book are also objects which reflect the interests of the mistress of the house and show her attitude toward the writer. They help the actress create the biography of her heroine and grow into her character.

It should be noted that an object can be of different importance to different characters. For instance, the photographs of the hostess's husband and children are very important to the writer. However, in this scene, they are of little importance to the mistress of the house. What is really important to her is her famous friend's dress, the book, and the newspaper clippings. The actor must always select only those objects that can help him to reveal the conflict and perform the action.

The choice of object is exceedingly important not only during the performance of an action. During a monolog, when the actor is alone on the stage, the object often bears a huge psychological load. For example, in the beginning of the play *The Cherry Orchard*, one of the play's characters, Lopakhin, appears on stage in a white vest and yellow shoes with a book in his hands. These objects help the actor create contrasts in mood: He has attained everything, has become almost a millionaire, while the book which he has been reading and could not understand, reminds him that he essentially remains the same illiterate peasant. Thus, the vest, the shoes and the book are extremely important objects, behind which Lopakhin's whole life is hidden, from his miserable childhood to his well-earned success. We have seen a production of *The Cherry Orchard* in which Lopakhin, due to the ill will of the director, muffled himself up in a blanket all the time. This object was not only unnecessary, it was a hindrance and detracted from the essence of the scene in which the smug new master Lopakhin prepares to meet the mistress of the house.

Emotional Memory

While exploring a role, said Stanislavsky, the actor often searches within himself for material, which he has experienced in life, and which is analogous to the character's feelings. These feelings do not belong to an imaginary person created by the author, but to the actor himself. Such a memory for previously experienced feelings is called an emotional memory.

Often, while describing a gripping event and reconstructing all of its particulars in his visual, auditory, muscular and other memory, a person revives in himself the previously experienced states of alarm, annoyance, joy, etc. with new force. In other words, through our sensory memory we influence our emotional memory.

The sensory memory and its related emotional recollections are of unique importance to the actor. They are the material that feeds his creativity. A true actor is one who has the ability to subtly see and hear, to grasp impressions vividly and retain them in his memory securely.

At the same time, Stanislavsky warned against attempting to address the emotional memory directly. He used to say that one cannot force oneself into one's subconscious with impunity and rummage around in it.[1] The emotions that are kept in our subconscious arise in us involuntarily, while recollecting images and events that have been imprinted on our visual, auditory, muscular, and other sensations. However, one cannot call forth emotions by a simple effort of the will. Such a violation of human nature leads the actor to internal dislocation and psychological strain.

It is not necessary for the actor himself to have been a

participant in the event that has brought forth these feelings. It can often happen that the emotional recollections are caused by an event of which the actor has only heard or read. When searching for internal material, one should use not only one's own life experience, but also that which we have seen in other people, with which we could sincerely identify. An analogous process occurs with recollections obtained from books, theatrical productions, movies and other people's stories. These impressions have to be processed within oneself into one's own genuine feelings, analogous to the feelings of the character in the play.

By way of personal example, I have retained a deep impression from a story I heard in childhood. I was told that a certain woman who lived in our apartment building was abandoned by her husband and suffered terribly. She sat motionless, with her husband's jacket thrown over her shoulders, and did not react to her surroundings. I was then a girl of twelve and this story amazed me. I pictured the woman very clearly and I was extremely sorry for her; I felt for her. If I were to have the occasion to play the abandoned woman, the prior emotional recollections would have helped me considerably.

The fact that the foundations of the conflicts that we examine always rest upon purely personal relations between people — how they declare themselves, how they impose upon one another — is extraordinarily conducive to the awakening of our emotional memory.

A substitution takes place involuntarily: I know I have already met with such a situation or such a person in life; I recognize this person or some of his traits in my friends or acquaintances. Long-forgotten memories of what I had felt during my encounter with this person may come back to me. Live images begin to appear in relation to this — how this person moved and talked, recollections of entire scenes or situations. Thus, in order for me to experience feelings analogous to my character's feelings, I make use of live material.

Entering the Stage

A character's life does not begin with the moment of his stage entrance: It is a continuation of something that has begun backstage. There are two types of stage entrances: the non-conflict situation and the conflict situation. In the non-conflict case, the character enters the stage without being in a state of conflict with anyone. He usually then begins to interact with a character (or characters). When entering the stage in a non-conflict situation, the actor must always know not only where he is coming from and why, but where he is going and why. For example, Jerome (*A Shocking Accident*) enters with the aim of finding out why he has been summoned and what the Headmaster wants of him. Afterwards, when he is already on the stage, Jerome engages in his conflict.

In the second case (a conflict situation), the characters appear while in the process of interaction; that is, continuing to perform their stage actions. Let us return to the improvisation, "The Old Uncle." Clearly, this scene is preceded by the scene in which the uncle meets his suddenly arrived nephew. Since we know that the uncle is deeply hurt by the fact that his nephew has neglected him for many years, we can assume that their conflict broke out immediately once they saw each other. That means that the process of interaction has started prior to "The Old Uncle" scene, and therefore, the characters enter the stage already in the state of conflict.

The problem is that the actors' behavior can't be natural if they enter the stage being "empty" and then begin to interact. The appropriate technique is to create an improvisation of the preceding scene with the given conflict and actions. Entering the stage in the process of performing this improvisation, the actors will provide a smooth and natural transition to the required scene.

The Actor's Attention On-stage

While the actor is playing his role on-stage, there is always the danger that he will lose the thread of his action or, if he is not involved in any conflict, the purpose of his physical activity. What to do in such a case? How to save the action, make it precise, and avoid losing it?

In such cases it is necessary to concentrate totally on the character, asking oneself: *Who* am I? *Where* am I? *What* am I doing, *why* and for what purpose? In order to restore better concentration, it is useful to narrow the circle of one's attention on-stage. Namely, the actor should concentrate his attention on the objects that are close to him. For example, the Headmaster's ruler (*A Shocking Accident*) could help him concentrate by twirling it and moving it from place to place.

When the actor feels ready to resume the escaping concentration, he can gradually return to his action. Then he can begin widening his "narrow" circle of attention, gradually encompassing everything that is taking place on-stage.

Chapter Four
Structuring the Play

Compared to a novel, a play is quite stark. There are none of the philosophical asides, descriptive passages or background explanations in a play, which help to reveal and understand the inner world of the characters in a novel. Only the words of the characters provide clues to their true motivations and intentions. However, as we have already noted repeatedly, the words of the characters are not valuable in themselves, but only as tokens of the larger reality which underlies them. The objective of director and actor is to understand why the author has endowed his characters with such exact words and not others; that is, to discover what conflicts and actions gave rise to such words.

Subdividing a Play into Events

In the previous chapters we have used examples of improvisations and a short story to show how to find the conflicts and actions. In each of these examples, there was only one conflict, and each of its participants performed only one action. In contrast to these examples, most plays contain numerous conflicts with the participation of many characters. However, every play can always be subdivided into a sequence of logically independent units, each of which has precisely one leading character who participates in only one conflict and performs only one action. Such a unit of the play we will call an *event*.

The merit of subdividing a play into events is that each of them can be analyzed independently from all the rest. (We must remember, though, that in order to find the given circumstances pertaining to an event, the whole play must be studied in its entirety.) At the same time, events are the indivisible "atoms" of the play: Any attempt to break down an event into smaller fragments leads to incorrect interpretation of the conflict between the characters.

Every event starts with the beginning of a conflict involving the leading character and ends when the leading character ends or changes his action. It follows that an event can end only in two ways: either the leading character achieves his objective in this conflict, or a new given circumstance appears which forces him to interrupt his action. In either case the event ends with the action of the leading character.

The end of an event does not necessarily mean an end to the given conflict. A play may have several successive events with the same conflict. Moreover, all those events may also have the same leading character if his actions change from event to event. Thus the basic principle of subdividing a play into events is observed as an event ends only when the action of the leading character ends.

It should be noted that the subdivision of a play into a series of successive events reflects the logic of the author and not one's own interpretation of the play. In this sense, a sequence of events exists objectively in any play; your task is to bring that sequence to the surface and make the obscure become apparent.

In order to show how to work on a concrete play, we have chosen an excerpt from Act I of the comedy *Even a Wise Man Stumbles* by Alexander Ostrovsky.

The events of the play take place in Russia in the late 1860s. A poor and talented young man, Glumov, has come to the conclusion that in order to achieve success in life, it is not enough to possess outstanding abilities — one must also make one's way into a circle of rich and influential people and obtain their patronage. As a first step, he decides to curry the favor of his rich uncle, Mamayev, and become indispensable in the latter's house. The matter is complicated by the fact that Mamayev has no liking for his numerous poor relations and wants nothing to do with them. However, he does have his weak points: According to one of the characters in the play, Mamayev "thinks he's the cleverest man alive, and he keeps teaching everyone. He likes nothing better than to give advice." Besides that, Mamayev likes to look at apartments that are for rent. Not that he has any need of new living quarters. He is not planning to move anywhere. It is only because such a pastime allows him to meet and talk with different people and bring happiness to them with his sage advice and homilies.

Having learned of Mamayev's weaknesses, Glumov bribed his servant into bringing his master to look at Glumov's apartment. Hearing the arrival of his uncle, whom he had never met before now, Glumov sends his mother into another room and sits down at his desk, pretending to be absorbed in work. The servant brings

Mamayev into the clean, well-furnished apartment.

Event One

MAMAYEV: *(Looks over the room without taking off his hat.)* This is a bachelor's apartment.

GLUMOV: *(Nods and continues to work.)* Yes, a bachelor's.

MAMAYEV: *(Not paying any attention)* It's not bad, but it is a bachelor's apartment. *(To the servant)* Where have you brought me to?

GLUMOV: *(Moves a chair and continues writing.)* Would you like to sit down?

MAMAYEV: *(Sits down.)* Thank you. Where have you brought me to, I ask you?

SERVANT: I'm sorry, Sir!

MAMAYEV: Don't you know what kind of apartment I want? You have to realize that I am a State Councilor, that my wife, your mistress, likes to keep an open house. We need a drawing-room — and not one! Where is the drawing-room, I ask you? *(To Glumov)* Please, excuse me!

GLUMOV: Not at all. You don't disturb me.

MAMAYEV: *(To the servant)* You see, there is a man writing! Perhaps we are in his way. Of course, he does not say so out of politeness. And it's all your fault, fool!

GLUMOV: Don't scold him: it's my fault, not his. On the staircase, when he was asking about an apartment, I recommended this one and said it was very good — I didn't know you were a family man.

MAMAYEV: Are you the tenant of this apartment?

GLUMOV: Yes.

MAMAYEV: Why are you leaving it?

GLUMOV: I can't afford it.

MAMAYEV: Why did you rent it, if you can't afford it? Who forced you? Did someone drag you by the collar, push you? Rent, rent! and now, up to your ears in debt? Eviction? Well, of course. From a large apartment to a single room, how pleasant will this be?

GLUMOV: No, I'd like to rent a larger one.

MAMAYEV: What do you mean larger? You can't afford this one and you are about to rent a larger one! What is the sense in it?

GLUMOV: No sense at all. Just stupidity.

MAMAYEV: Stupidity? What nonsense!

GLUMOV: It's not nonsense! I'm just stupid.

Conflict and Actions

In order to determine the conflict, it is first necessary to identify the leading character, and then find the circumstances which induce the leading character to begin the confrontation and which determine the led character's response. As a rule, the circumstances for the leading character can be found either immediately before the event or in its very beginning.

It should be remembered, however, that the circumstances themselves do not yet lead to personal confrontations between the characters. For that to occur, it is necessary for a character to find a certain something in them which cannot leave him indifferent and which forms in him a certain opinion concerning either himself or his opponent.

Therefore, in order to identify such circumstances we must understand how they are perceived by the sides of the conflict; we must view them through their own eyes in their own interpretation. In that case, the description of the given circumstances will already contain the logic and mind-set of the corresponding character. Needless to say, this interpretation must be based on the material of the play and not on one's unrestricted imagination.

Leading Character

The leading character in this event is Glumov: He originates and sustains the conflict, which would immediately die without his efforts. Glumov's main given circumstance is that Mamayev likes to lecture everyone. Therefore, in order to make Mamayev interested in him, Glumov decides to present himself as an ideal object for lecturing, that is, a simple and artless person, who does not completely realize what he is doing. This is the position which Glumov has thought up for himself in his conflict with Mamayev.

And what is the action that Glumov uses in order to convince Mamayev? It is easy to see that his action consists of flabbergasting Mamayev, astounding him with his illogicality and eccentricity — confusing him. While performing his action, Glumov continuously puts Mamayev at a loss, thus keeping him "warmed up" and providing him with new grounds for lecturing. He first breaks all the rules of etiquette by paying almost no attention to Mamayev's arrival, he doesn't even greet him, and then he babbles some nonsense about moving to a larger apartment.

Please note that, while "taunting" Mamayev, Glumov makes

sure not to accidentally go too far and totally offend his uncle. He behaves politely, offers him a chair, then takes the servant's fault upon himself and apologizes.

The Led Character

What has caused Mamayev to enter the struggle? What circumstance pushed him into a confrontation with Glumov? Such a circumstance was the outrageous behavior of the apartment owner: He not only found it unnecessary to get up and greet Mamayev, on whose face it is written that he is an important person, but he also continues with his personal work, paying almost no attention to Mamayev's presence. Mamayev's pride has been wounded, and he is not planning to silently put up with such a disrespectful attitude towards himself.

Mamayev sees Glumov as a spoiled, ill-mannered young man, one of these modern youngsters who have no respect for elders, thinking that they can live by their own wits. This is his side in the conflict. Accordingly, Mamayev's action is to teach Glumov a lesson, to tick him off. However, no matter how much indignation Mamayev feels, he cannot lower himself to showing that he is hurt. Therefore, he reprimands Glumov as though addressing himself to his servant.

Let us note that there is no conflict between the servant and Mamayev: They are not trying to get anything from each other, neither of them is trying to impose upon the other. Mamayev is using the servant as an object, as a tool: Everything he says to the servant is actually addressed to Glumov. Mamayev is completely indifferent to how the servant perceives his words and what he says to him in response. The servant, who has just received a bribe from Glumov, also has no reason for entering into a conflict with Mamayev and imposing anything upon him. He simply answers in a formal manner, as required to do: "I am sorry, Sir."

Energy

Glumov is trying not to pay too much attention to the newcomer, and he restrains the flow of energy that is ready to pour onto the uncle. He would have lunged at his uncle with an embrace, but the uncle does not like poor relatives. Mamayev, on the other hand, is indignant over the young man's disrespectful behavior, and not feeling obliged to restrain himself, freely directs his energy onto him.

Determining the End of the Event

As noted before, the principle of breaking a play down into events requires that each event involve only one leading character that has only one conflict and one action. Correspondingly, an event can end only in two ways: Either the leading character achieves his objective in this conflict or a new given circumstance appears which forces him to interrupt his action.

In this scene, it is the first case which prevails: Glumov himself ends his action and, therefore, the event. He has successfully executed his plan. His foolishness and illogicality have amazed Mamayev.

Event Two

MAMAYEV: Stupid? That's strange. What do you mean by that?

GLUMOV: Very simple — I don't have enough brains. What's so strange about it? It happens quite often.

MAMAYEV: Well, this is interesting! A man calls himself stupid.

GLUMOV: What else can I do? Wait until others tell me I am? Does it make any difference? It can't be hidden anyway.

MAMAYEV: Well, it's very difficult to hide this deficiency indeed.

GLUMOV: So I'm not hiding it.

MAMAYEV: I'm sorry for you.

GLUMOV: Thank you very much.

MAMAYEV: Perhaps, you don't have anyone to teach you?

GLUMOV: No, I don't.

Conflict and Actions

In this event, the leading character is Mamayev. An incredible, improbable case: For the first time in his life Mamayev has met a man who confesses to his own stupidity. Mamayev is thrown off guard, becomes suspicious — such a thing cannot be! Is not the stranger playing some kind of a trick?

This circumstance defines Mamayev's position in the conflict: For him Glumov is an eccentric, an odd and incomprehensible fellow. Therefore, Mamayev's action consists of sounding out, looking into and determining what kind of "bird" he has before him. He carefully and curiously studies this extraordinary young man, not knowing whether he can believe him or not.

Glumov's given circumstance is that his uncle is dismayed, does not know how to react, treats him warily and with mistrust. Accordingly, Glumov continues to impose upon Mamayev the same as before. Namely, that he is simple and frank and that he says what he thinks. He is not planning to dissemble or hide anything — it would be useless, and besides, he does not even know how to do it.

However, Glumov's action is now entirely different: It is to divert the uncle's suspicion and mistrust. Glumov "does not understand" that Mamayev is checking him out. He has clear eyes and a wide smile. This man is not hiding anything — he is even incapable of concealing anything.

As usual, the event ends with the termination of the leading character's action. Mamayev has finally determined the reason for the odd behavior and incredible assertions of this actually decent young man. It turns out that he has no one who could direct him in life, from whom he could learn all there is to know. There is nothing more to elucidate, and Mamayev terminates his action.

Energy

Mamayev restrains the flow of energy, which is ready to burst out onto the partner. Although this unusual young man interests him, he still treads warily, being careful not to fall into a trap. Is it possible that he is being laughed at? Glumov is the embodiment of candor itself; his energy flows freely onto the uncle.

Event Three

MAMAYEV: But there are teachers, very clever teachers, but no one pays any attention to them, such are the times. Well, you can't expect anything from the old people: Everyone thinks that if he is old he must be wise. But when the boys are disobedient, what can you expect of them afterwards? Let me tell you one case. A schoolboy recently was nearly running on the way home from school. I, of course, stopped and gave him, just as a joke, a little homily: To school you walk slowly, but you run back home — it should be, my dear, just the other way around. Another one would be grateful that a respectable person stops in the street because of him. And what did he say?

GLUMOV: Nowadays, you know, teaching is …

MAMAYEV: "We are sick and tired of being lectured at school. If you like to teach, get a job at our school. And now, let me go, I am hungry!" A boy, saying this to me!

GLUMOV: That boy is on the dangerous path. I feel sorry for him! Yes, after all of this, I think, you feel unpleasant.

MAMAYEV: *(Sternly)* Please, don't remind me of it, I beg you. I felt at the time as if something pierced me right here. *(Points to his*

chest.) And even now, I feel as if something like a stake is
sticking there ...

GLUMOV: Here?

MAMAYEV: A little higher.

GLUMOV: Here?

MAMAYEV: *(Angrily)* Higher, I told you!

GLUMOV: Excuse me, please! Don't be angry! I told you that I was
stupid.

Conflict and Actions

This scene is again led by Mamayev. Luck has definitely been
with Mamayev today: He has met a man with a virgin state of mind,
splendid material for lecturing. This gives rise to his side of the
conflict. Mamayev sees Glumov as a naive youngster, who does not
understand anything in life, to whom everything has to be
explained, everything has to be taught, a fool who does not realize
what is going on around him. Mamayev's action is to enlighten, to
acquaint Glumov with reality. He shows him a couple of examples
of the sorry state into which modern society has fallen and points
out the cause of all ills: free thinking and disdain for the experience
of elders. After speaking out once more on his favorite topics,
Mamayev ends his action.

Glumov's given circumstance is that the uncle has taken the bait
and has begun to lecture him. Now it is possible to try to establish
closer contact with him, to become more intimate with him.
Accordingly, now Glumov's position is that he holds the same
views as Mamayev, that he totally agrees with his uncle.

Glumov's action is to avoid a blunder, to please and encourage
Mamayev. Glumov seconds Mamayev's opinions, expressing his
utmost understanding and agreement — he thinks exactly like his
uncle.

Energy

Mamayev directs a free flow of energy at his partner — he
pours out his heart. Glumov is completely open — all of his energy
is directed towards his partner. He is enjoying himself, absorbing
everything that he hears. He is all ears, afraid to miss even a single
word coming from the lips of this wise man.

Event Four

MAMAYEV: Yes, you are stupid ... That's bad. That is, there is
nothing wrong with it, if you have elderly, experienced

relatives or acquaintances.

GLUMOV: The trouble is that I have nobody. I have my mother, but she's even more stupid than I.

MAMAYEV: Your situation is truly bad. I'm sorry for you, young man.

GLUMOV: They say I have an uncle, but it is just as if he doesn't exist.

MAMAYEV: Why is that?

GLUMOV: He doesn't know me, and I have no desire to meet him.

MAMAYEV: I can't praise you for that, young man. I can't.

GLUMOV: But, please, understand me! If he were a poor man, I'd be glad to kiss his hands. But he's rich — if I were to come to him for advice, he'd think that I'd come for his money. How can I convince him that I don't want a penny of his, that I'm just craving for his advice, dying for his guidance. I heard he is a man of exceptional wisdom. I'd be ready to listen to him day and night.

MAMAYEV: You're not as stupid as you say.

GLUMOV: At times something comes over me, suddenly I am brighter, but then I am back to my normal self. Most of the time I hardly know what I'm doing. That's when I need advice.

MAMAYEV: And who is your uncle?

GLUMOV: I've almost forgotten his name. Nil Mamayev, I believe.

Conflict and Actions

Mamayev leads. The young man has again reminded him that he needs a mentor. Mamayev is inspired and thirsts for action. The young man's candor and intelligent views make him attractive to Mamayev, and he is ready to take Glumov under his guidance immediately. Mamayev's side in the conflict is that he sees Glumov as a pleasant young man with innate ability, who could go far if guided properly.

Mamayev's action is to guide, to enter Glumov's life. Mamayev enjoys his role of mentor. He talks to Glumov in a peremptory manner, as though knowing that all of his judgments are infallible. The appearance of a new given circumstance — Mamayev learns that Glumov is his nephew — interrupts his stage action and, at the same time, terminates the current event.

Glumov's given circumstance is that everything is proceeding smoothly according to plan — the uncle is obviously interested in him, is even offering himself as a mentor. An extremely favorable ground has been created. Now it is possible to play on his feelings. Glumov's side in the conflict consists of presenting himself as a shy, unselfish young man, lonely and lost in a world he does not understand. He is lost without guidance and does not understand where to go or what to do in life.

Glumov's action is to warm up interest in himself and arouse trust. He draws Mamayev into the circle of his "unhappy" life and at the same time stresses his complete unselfishness.

Energy

Mamayev directs a free flow of energy at his partner. It is his luck to have come across such a wonderful pupil. As before, Glumov's entire energy is directed at Mamayev.

Event Five

MAMAYEV: And who are you?

GLUMOV: Glumov.

MAMAYEV: Son of Dimitrii Glumov?

GLUMOV: That's correct.

MAMAYEV: Well, that Mamayev is I.

GLUMOV: Oh, my goodness! How is it possible? No, no! Please, give me your hand! *(Almost in tears)* But, uncle, I've heard that you don't like your relatives; don't worry, we can be as distant as before. I will not dare to visit you without your order. It is enough that I have seen you and enjoyed a conversation with a wise man.

MAMAYEV: Not at all. Come and see me when you are in need of advice.

GLUMOV: When I am in need of it! I am in constant need of advice, every single minute! I feel I'll perish without a mentor!

MAMAYEV: Well, come and see me tonight.

GLUMOV: Thank you very much! Let me introduce you to my old mother. She's not clever, but she's a kind, very kind woman.

MAMAYEV: Well, why not?

GLUMOV: *(Aloud)* Mother! *(Enter Glumov's mother.)*

Conflict and Actions

Mamayev leads. Everything has come out perfectly: This nice young man has turned out to be his nephew. The cross-examination has shown that Glumov is modest, unselfish, holds correct views, values intelligent people and thirsts for guidance. Mamayev likes the young man and is ready to take him into his retinue, let him into his home.

Mamayev sees himself as a good uncle who has the warmest feelings of affection for his kinsman Glumov. This is his side of the conflict. Mamayev's action is to draw near, to treat his newly-found nephew with affection. Where else will he find such an ideal pupil?

Glumov's given circumstance — Success! Mamayev has owned up to their kinship himself. However, this in itself is not enough. The uncle does not allow his numerous poor relations near him; Glumov must now force his way into the uncle's house. Glumov continues the game, imposing his side of the conflict. For him, Mamayev continues to be an unapproachable person. They are divided by such great distance, that he cannot even dream of them becoming intimate. Glumov's action is to pin his uncle down, to prevent his retreat.

Note that in order to strengthen their kinship, Glumov immediately introduces his mother to Mamayev. The event ends with the appearance of a new given circumstance — the entrance of Glumov's mother.

Energy
Both Mamayev and Glumov are overwhelmed with happiness, and each one of them freely directs his energy out onto his partner.

On the Character's Position in a Conflict
We would like to point out an interesting feature of the play *Even a Wise Man Stumbles*: Throughout the entire play Glumov changes his appearance like a chameleon, depending on the person with whom he is interacting. With each character in the play, Glumov plays a particular role that helps him gain the other's affection and trust. Accordingly, Glumov "makes up" his own positions in his conflicts. His conflicts thus differ from the examples we have examined in the previous chapters, where the characters entered a struggle in order to stand up for what they honestly believed. Glumov does not impose upon his opponents that which he believes himself, but that which will, in his opinion, further the realization of his plans. For example, in the events of the play that we have just analyzed, Glumov's plan is to penetrate into Mamayev's home.

Thus, the character is not at all obliged to "believe" in whatever he is trying to convince his opponent. His position in the conflict is determined not necessarily by what he believes, but by what he considers to be advantageous for himself under the given circumstances.

Possible Types of Conflicts in an Event

In this book, we are looking at only the simplest type of conflict, namely that which involves only two characters. But in the most general case, either side or both sides of the conflict may involve several characters.

If the leading side of the conflict consists of several characters, they must all perform in the given conflict as an entity. They must all hold the same position vis-à-vis the opposing side of the conflict and perform the same action. However, if the led side of the conflict includes several characters, each of them may have his own position in the conflict as well as his own action.

Conflict relations between characters are not limited to the case of confrontation between two sides. Besides the main conflict, which defines the beginning and the end of an event, an event may also include a number of additional conflicts; the leading character of the main conflict cannot be involved in these additional conflicts.[1]

The Concept of the Superobjective

Stanislavsky pointed out that in a play each character has some overall objective or main desire, which conditions the character's behavior throughout the entire play. Stanislavsky called this desire "the superobjective of the character." The striving towards the superobjective is what brings all parts of the role together and determines its development in the direction given by the author. It is extremely useful for the actor to know the superobjective of his role, since this enables him to create an integral and purposeful theatrical character.

But, what is the meaning of the superobjective? What kind of character's desire does it represents? To answer this question it is necessary to recall that the essence of each character is revealed through his interaction with other characters, through the conflicts in which he is involved. Therefore, each of these conflicts must contribute to the character's main desire and be a step towards attaining his superobjective.

As we know, in any conflict a character strives to impose a certain opinion about himself or his opponent. In either case, it allows him to reveal himself and demonstrate what he is. The only difference is that in the former case the character explicitly states his opinion of himself, while in the latter he does this obliquely, revealing himself through his perception of his opponent. Therefore, in each separate conflict the character tries to influence his opponent's view of him in order to be accepted in the manner he desires. At the same time, each of these conflicts contributes to the character's self-image, which he is building throughout the whole play. Clearly, this self-image is what Stanislavsky called "the superobjective."

From the foregoing it follows that the superobjective of the character always has to be sought in the sphere of the character's relations with others. Therefore, the character cannot have a superobjective, for example, such as: "I wish to be a scientist." Whether he is a scientist or not is given by the playwright, and nothing can change this fact. However, the character can impose upon his partners that he is a scientist (no matter whether it is true or false) and, consequently, his superobjective really will be: "I wish to be regarded as a scientist."

Stanislavsky provides two examples of such erroneously formulated superobjectives.[2] Playing the role of Argan in *The Imaginary Invalid (Le Malade Imaginaire)* by Molière, he first defined his superobjective as "I wish to be sick." Despite all of Stanislavsky's efforts, the role did not come out: He went further and further away from comedy to pathology, to the tragedy of illness. The role took shape only when Stanislavsky discovered another definition for the superobjective: "I wish to be *regarded* as a sick man."

In another play, *Mistress of the Inn (La Locandiera)* by Goldoni, Stanislavsky first defined his superobjective as "I wish to avoid women," but the role then lost its wittiness. The role livened up only after Stanislavsky came to realize that his hero (the Cavaliere Rippafratta) is a lover of women, who simply wants to pass for a misogynist. This helped define the superobjective as: "I wish to be *regarded* as a misogynist."

However, it is not an easy task to determine the superobjective of a given character. It is rarely possible to encompass an entire role and identify its superobjective without a detailed analysis of the play. As we review all the events involving the given character we strive to detect a certain trend and guess how the character wants to be accepted by other characters of the play. Knowledge of the superobjective is very important, because it allows one to verify the accuracy of the constructed conflicts while analyzing the play. This means that if in a particular event the character's behavior is not directed towards the achievement of an already identified superobjective, or even worse, contradicts that striving, it usually means some mistake has been made in analyzing the given event.

From the above it follows that we cannot determine the superobjectives of Glumov and Mamayev simply on the basis of the five events from the play which we have just analyzed. However, since the authors had analyzed the entire play, they know the superobjectives. A careful study of the role of Glumov leads to conclusions that throughout the play he strives to make people see him as a straightforward and earnest person, who always says what he thinks. Mamayev sees himself as a person filled with worldly wisdom. This is his superobjective, this is how he wants to be perceived by others.

An example of how to find the superobjectives for all of the characters in the play, Chekhov's *The Cherry Orchard*, can be found in our book *Working on the Play and the Role*.

Chapter Five
Work on a Monolog

The monolog is the act of talking to oneself or thinking aloud, i.e., the soliloquy. Through the monolog the author makes it possible for the audience to understand what preoccupies the character, what oppresses him, invades his thoughts. Through the monolog, a character reveals some of his inner world, his hidden thoughts. The important point is that during a monolog the character does not interact with anyone and consequently is not involved in any conflict and has no stage action. In this case it doesn't matter whether the character is on the stage alone or in the company of other characters.

It should be noted, however, that in Webster's Dictionary the word "monolog" has yet another definition: a long speech by one speaker. This dual use of the word "monolog" often leads to misconception and confusion. In particular, during auditions student actors quite often perform a portion of dialog calling it "monolog." They either ignore the existence of partners or they address their words to imaginary partners. The first is incorrect, since each dialog implies an interaction between characters: The character to whom a speech is addressed does not simply wait his turn to speak but constantly evaluates his partner's words, and with his whole physical behavior engages in a silent struggle with him.[1] The second—addressing to imaginary partners—is totally devoid of meaning, since it is impossible to envisage how an imaginary partner will counteract. Stanislavsky used to tell his students: "Interaction with a dead object is highly harmful. You should be getting something from the object and be dependent on it. It is impossible to interact with a live object in an imaginary fashion."[2]

Since in the course of a monolog the actor does not interact with anyone, there is always a danger that the monolog will lack inner development, become lifeless, and degenerate into just a static declamation in which the absence of action is masked by an emotional embellishment of words. In order to give the monolog inner development and movement, it is necessary to find its contrasts, juxtapositions, and contradictions, which reflect the internal struggle of the character.

This internal struggle arises as a result of a clash between contradictory thoughts, ideas, desires. The hero poses questions to himself and tries to answer them. He presents for his own consideration something that has its pros and cons, its positive and negative sides, which necessitates either defense or denial.

The actor's objective is to find the essence of these contradictions; namely, what his character wants, what he is trying to suppress within himself in connection with the desire and of what he is trying to convince himself. Only then will the actor be able to construct a process for solving the character's problems on the stage.

Technically, this is achieved by means of dividing the monolog into a succession of segments, wherein each segment reflects one of the stages of the internal argument that the character carries on with himself. Each segment should contain a certain idea that would be in juxtaposition to the main idea of the previous segment.

A segment can be of any length. It can even consist of only one phrase, and it is dedicated to the solution of one contradiction. It should be noted that the contradiction of any given segment does not arise in the beginning of it. The objection, the new idea, ripens in the course of the previous segment and as a result, a new segment materializes. A pause may often separate the new segment from the previous. However, it is not obligatory — having reached a new decision, the character can abruptly interrupt the current segment and begin a new one.

The character's contradictions do not arise with the first words of the monolog. When he begins the monolog, he already carries these contradictions within himself. A monolog is the continuation and the development of an argument with oneself. Therefore, the actor must guess at what arguments and thoughts had arisen in his character before the monolog began, so that the first piece of the monolog would be in contrast to them. These arguments must naturally be based on the given circumstances of the character. These circumstances often appear shortly before the beginning of the monolog. However, as in the case of the conflict, the author may inform us of these circumstances at any point in the play.

Variations in the flow of energy during a monolog can be

determined on the basis of the established sequence of segments. Every new juxtaposition changes the direction of the energy flow.

Below we will examine three examples of a monolog: the monolog of Natalya Petrovna in Ivan Turgenev's comedy *A Month in the Country*, of the King in Shakespeare's tragedy *Hamlet, Prince of Denmark* and of Podkolesin in Nikolai Gogol's *The Marriage*.

Monolog of Natalya Petrovna from *A Month in the Country*

The first step in working on a monolog is to choose the given circumstances that are relevant:

Natalya Petrovna, a cultured twenty-nine-year-old woman, is married to a kind and rich landowner, Arkady. The country life is eventless and boring, and Natalya Petrovna entertains herself by flirting with a family friend, Rakitin, who is in love with her. Her son has a charming twenty-one-year-old tutor, Belyayev; and without being aware of it, Natalya Petrovna falls madly in love with him. She believes that Belyayev, who becomes flustered and doesn't know how to conduct himself in her presence, is also attracted to her. However, in Natalya Petrovna's household there is her seventeen-year-old ward, Vera, who spends most of her time with Belyayev, talking with him all the time.

Suspecting that Vera is attracted to Belyayev, Natalya Petrovna uses a pretext that their middle-aged neighbor wants to make a proposal of marriage to Vera, in order to engage her in a candid talk. During the conversation, Natalya Petrovna draws out a confession from Vera that she is head over heels in love with Belyayev and that she believes he reciprocates her feelings. Hearing this, Natalya Petrovna suddenly pales, breaks off the conversation and asks Vera to leave her alone. Here follows Natalya Petrovna's monolog:[3]

> **1.** *(Natalya Petrovna remains alone for some time, motionless.)* Now everything is clear to me ... These children love each other. *(She stops and passes her hand over her face.)* Well, so much the better. God grants them happiness! *(Laughing)* And I ... I might have thought ... *(She stops again.)* **2.** She blurted it out very quickly ... I confess I never suspected ... I confess this news overwhelmed me ... But just wait. It isn't all over yet. **3.** Good Heavens, what am I saying? What's the matter with me? I don't recognize myself. What have I come to? *(After a pause)* What am I doing? I am trying to marry a poor little girl ... to an old man! ... *(She trembles and suddenly raises her head.)* But what does this mean, really? Am I jealous of Vera? Am I ... am I

in love with him? *(After a pause)* **4.** And do you still doubt it? You are in love, unhappy woman! How this happened, I do not know. It is as if I had been given poison … **5.** Suddenly all is crushed, shattered, swept away … He is afraid of me … What does he care for me? … What use has he for such a creature as I? He is young, and she is young. And I? *(Bitterly)* How can he appreciate me? … *(Rises.)* **6.** Really, it seems to me, I am going mad. Why exaggerate? Well, yes, I am overwhelmed … This is a new thing to me. This is the first time that I … Yes, the first time! I am in love now for the first time! *(She sits down again.)* **7.** He must go away. Yes, and Rakitin too. It's time for me to come to my senses. Here's what I have come to. And what is it that I like in him? *(Meditates.)* So here it is, that frightful emotion … Arkady! Yes, I will run to his embrace. I will implore him to forgive me, to defend me, to save me — he … and no one else. All other men are strangers to me, and must remain strangers … **8.** But, is it possible … is it possible there is no other means? That little girl, she is only a child. She may have been mistaken. This is all childishness, after all … Why did I … ? I will have an explanation with him myself. I will ask him … **9.** *(With a reproach)* Ah, ah? Do you still have hope? Do you still desire to have hope? And what do I hope for! Good God, do not let me despise myself! *(She leans her head on her hands.)*

The very first segment should already contain a certain juxtaposition: Specifically, it should contain an answer to the thought, which had occurred to the character even before the monolog began. In this particular monolog, the first segment is an answer to Natalya Petrovna's thought: "What a surprise that Belyayev is in love with Vera! I would never have thought it." (Natalya Petrovna is stunned by that discovery—she is bubbling with energy and ready to explode.)

Following are nine segments, each of which is juxtaposed to the thought that is expressed in the preceding segment.

1. It's wonderful that Belyayev is in love with Vera and not with me. Now everything has been settled in the best possible manner. I am simply happy for them. (In this segment, Natalya Petrovna makes a great effort to suppress her energy and pronounce the first phrase of the monolog.)

2. And yet I hope that nothing will come of it. (She lost control of her energy, and it escapes.)

3. But why I am against it? No, I can't believe that I am jealous of Vera, that I am in love with Belyayev. (Natalya Petrovna restrains the flow of energy.)

4. But that is precisely the case — I am in love with him. (The energy bursts out: Natalya Petrovna cannot control it.)

5. Still, why do I need this love? It will only bring me grief, since I cannot hope that he returns my affection. (She regains control of her energy, pushes it back.)

6. But, on the other hand, it is impossible simply to deny such a new and exciting feeling! (The energy trickles out.)

7. No, it would be better to cure myself of this illness — send Belyayev away and find peace and oblivion in the bosom of my family. (The energy is pushed back again.)

8. But should I really part with Belyayev? Why should I believe Vera? I must find out for myself whether he is in love with her. (The energy continues to slip away.)

9. What kind of behavior am I exhibiting! My passion is making me stoop down to lowly intrigues. (Natalya Petrovna forces the flow of energy back.)

Monolog of the King from *Hamlet, Prince of Denmark*

The given circumstance is that The King has committed a terrible crime — fratricide. The thought of it pursues him relentlessly, does not give him a single moment of peace.

1. Oh, my offence is rank, it smells to heaven;
     It hath the primal eldest curse upon't —
     A brother's murder! Pray can I not,
     Through inclination be as sharp as will,
     My stronger guilt defeats my strong intent,
     And, like a man to double business bound,
     I stand in pause where I shall first begin,
     And both neglect. 2. What if this cursed hand
     Were thicker than itself with brother's blood,
     Is there not rain enough in the sweet heavens
     To wash it white as snow? Whereto serves mercy
     But to confront the visage of offence?
     And what's in prayer but this twofold force,
     To be forestalled ere we come to fall
     Or pardoned being down? Then I'll look up.
     My fault is past. 3. But oh, what form of prayer
     Can serve my turn? 'Forgive me my foul murder'?

That cannot be, since I am still possessed
Of those effects for which I did the murder —
My crown, my own ambitions, and my queen.
May one be pardoned and retain th'offence?
4. In the corrupted currents of this world
Offence's gilded hand may shove by justice,
And oft'tis seen the wicked prize itself
Buys out the law. But 'tis not so above:
There is no shuffling, there the action lies
In his true nature, and we ourselves compelled
Even to the teeth and forehead of our faults
To give in evidence. What then? What rests?
Try what repentance can. What can it not?
5. Yet what can it, when one cannot repent?
6. O wretched state! O bosom black as death!
O limed soul, that struggling to be free
Art more engaged! Help, angels! Make assay.
Bow, stubborn knees; and heart with strings of steel,
Be soft as sinews of the new-born babe.
All may be well. *(He kneels.)*
7. My words fly up, my thoughts remain below.
Words without thoughts never to heaven go.

First, it is necessary to determine which thoughts in the character's mind preceded the monolog, so that his very first words would be in response and in contrast to them. This technique immediately gives movement to the monolog.

The thought is: "Through prayer I must cleanse my soul of sin!" (The King does not really believe in such an outcome; he pumps up his energy.) In answer to this thought comes the first segment:

1. The King cannot force himself to pray, because he understands the futility of prayer. The crime is so horrible that it cannot be absolved. There simply are no prayers powerful enough to expiate the sin of fratricide! (In this segment, his energy is slipping away.)

   However, such a conclusion does not suit the King. While he utters his words, objections are gradually forming in his head. Accordingly, a new segment of the monolog is initiated.

2. Hasn't the King lost hope prematurely? One of the purposes of prayer is precisely to save the soul of the sinner after the sin has been committed. (He pushes forth the flow of energy.)

However, while uttering these words, the King gradually realizes that he doesn't understand what form such a prayer should take, in order for it to be efficacious. He expresses his doubts in the following segment.

3. It is futile to hope for absolution while the King continues to enjoy the fruits of his ambitious crime — his crown, his queen — which he is not planning to give up! (The energy escapes.)

4. However, the King continues to search for a way out: Unfortunately, the Heavens cannot be bribed and it is useless to dissemble with them ... What means are left, then, to win them over? Ah, he has found a way — sincere repentance! (The King is compelled to produce energy within himself.)

5. But, speaking of repentance, the King realizes that not only does he not repent of anything, he enjoys all that he has achieved. So this path to salvation is also closed to him! (His energy disperses, slips away.)

6. But the King is not ready to give up. Perhaps not everything is lost yet — he will take hold of himself, he will force himself to repent! The King makes a desperate attempt to find repentance within himself. (Another effort to produce energy.)

7. The King comes to the conclusion that all his attempts are futile, that he is incapable of repentance. (All his energy disappeared; nothing is left.)

Monolog of Podkolesin from *The Marriage*

A confirmed bachelor, Podkolesin has long dreamed of getting married but cannot bring himself to take such a desperate step. At Podkolesin's request, his friend introduces him into a house where there is a pretty girl of marriageable age. Seeing that Podkolesin cannot get up his courage to propose to the girl, the friend proposes on his behalf. The girl accepts the proposal and Podkolesin demands that they go to church and get married immediately, without waiting a single moment. Everyone leaves the room to prepare for the trip, and Podkolesin is left alone in the room. Here follows Podkolesin's monolog:[4]

1. What have I been till now, in reality? Did I understand the significance of life? I didn't. I understood nothing. What, what has my bachelor life been like? What was I good for? What did I do? I went on from day to day, did my work, went to the office, ate my dinner, and went to sleep — in fact, I've been the most frivolous and ordinary

man in the world. Only now one sees how stupid everyone is who doesn't get married; yet if you come to think of it, what numbers of men go on living in blindness. If I were a king, I would order everyone to be married: absolutely everyone, so that there shouldn't be one bachelor in my kingdom. When one thinks, you know, in a few minutes one will be married! All at once, one will taste bliss such as is only to be found in fairy tales, which there's no expressing, nor finding words to express. *(After a brief pause)* **2.** But, say what you will, it is positively alarming when one thinks it over. To bind oneself for all one's life, for all one's days, come what may, and no getting out of it afterwards, no retracting it, nothing, nothing — everything over, everything settled. Why, even now it's impossible to turn back; in another minute I shall be in church: It's quite impossible to get away — there's the carriage there already and everything prepared. **3.** But is it really impossible to get away? Why, naturally it's impossible. There are people standing there, and at the door and everywhere. Why, they'll ask what for? I cannot. No! But here's an open window. What about the window? No, I can't; why, to be sure, it's undignified; besides, it's a long way down to the ground … *(Goes up to the window.)* **4.** Oh well, it's not so high: There's only the one floor, and that's a low one. **5.** Oh no, how could I: I don't have even a cap. How can I go without a hat? So awkward! **6.** Though, after all, can't I go without a hat? What if I were to try, eh? Shall I try? *(Stands on the window, and saying, "Lord help me!" jumps into the street; is heard moaning and groaning below.)* Oh, it was a long way, though. Hi, cabman! Off! Off!

Podkolesin's thought before the monolog begins: "I am immensely terrified! It's better to get married quickly, before doubts enter my head, so that I won't change my mind!" In answer to this thought comes the first segment of the monolog. (Podkolesin shrinks with fear, his energy flow is directed inside his body.)

1. Podkolesin tries to convince himself that it is foolish for him to fear anything, that it is foolish to clutch at his meaningless bachelor existence: there is nothing for him to regret. (During the segment, Podkolesin makes great efforts to produce energy and overcome impediments.)
2. But, on the other hand, perhaps he is overrating the virtues of family life? Who knows how it could yet turn out! Perhaps

he is committing an irreparable mistake. (His energy is dispersing.)

3. However, that is not to be thought of now! Everything is ready for the wedding and there is no going back! (Podkolesin pushes forth the energy.)
4. But perhaps the situation is not so totally hopeless? Perhaps he can still run away? (The energy slips away again.)
5. He could run away, but it would be somewhat improper to appear on the street without a hat. (The last weak attempt to pump up his energy.)
6. Really, now is not the time to think of proprieties! He must save himself! (There is no energy left.)

Chapter Six
The Actor's Training

It is not enough to understand and learn the stated method of working on the role in theory, in the abstract: The method must be grasped practically, felt, must become part of everyday life. One has to reorganize his way of thinking in such a way as to always search behind the characters' words for their personal conflicts and their perceptions of each other, to see what they wish to impose upon their opponent and how they do it. It means that the actor must learn to visualize each day in his life as a continuous chain of actions performed by others, to become adept at interpreting relationships between people, understanding the essence of what they are imposing upon each other in uttering words or in keeping silent.

Begin your training with an analysis of scenes from your everyday life which have stayed in your mind, which have attracted your attention by their oddity, absurdity, artlessness, humor, etc. You will always find time for such an analysis, either during free moments throughout the course of the day or in the evening when you are getting ready to sleep, as the images of the past day or of the distant past run through your mind. Such daily training is the first step towards becoming a professional.

Following are several examples of real-life scenes that have caught our attention.

1. The Grapefruits
I remember an elderly couple, neighbors of ours, who were on a grapefruit diet. I, too, decided to try this diet and went to the wholesale market to buy some grapefruits cheaply, having promised to share them with our neighbors. But my first purchase was unsuccessful — the grapefruits turned out to be sour and I threw them away. Later, in order to avoid lengthy explanations on a trivial subject, I simply told my neighbors that my market idea had not worked out. However, for a long time afterwards the neighbors

continued to ask me how I liked grapefruits from the wholesale market and whether they were better than the ones in the supermarket, and each time I had to repeat to them that I no longer go to the wholesale market. I continued to be somewhat surprised by such odd forgetfulness on their part, but chalked it up to their advanced age and decided not to pay any attention to the matter.

Once, during a visit with my neighbors, I noticed that while asking me about the grapefruits, they nudged each other imperceptibly. It became clear to me right away that all this while they had not believed me about not going to the market, but had thought that I simply did not want to share my grapefruits with them. I immediately invited the neighbors over to my home and treated them to some grapefruits, which I bought in the same supermarket they did.

When I subsequently analyzed our relations, I discovered that two successive conflicts had taken place between us. In both conflicts my neighbors were the leading side, acting as an entity, as a group. They presented themselves as perceptive characters who could see through me. Their action likewise remained constant: It consisted in showing me up, in exposing me.

My positions and actions differed in both conflicts. In the beginning, when I did not understand their motivation, the sole circumstance which determined my side of the conflict was their asking me the same thing over and over again. Accordingly, I saw them as senile, forgetful people, and my action consisted in reminding them, in refreshing their memory.

However, as soon as the leading side presented me with a new given circumstance — that they hadn't believed me all this time — my attitude towards them changed: I saw them as people who had been mistaken about me. In offering them some grapefruits, I performed my action: to smooth over our relations.

This story is remarkable for its ordinariness: In life we constantly find ourselves engaged in conflicts that have arisen as a result of mutual misunderstanding.

2. The Incident in Arezzo

It is particularly useful to analyze situations in which, in our opinion, people behaved strangely and illogically. In such cases we are forced to look at circumstances from a new and unusual point of view.

We once stayed in a hotel in Arezzo, a small Italian city far from the usual tourist itineraries. Leafing through our passports, the clerk at the desk threw a suspicious glance at us and said, "Something is wrong with your passports." "And what could that be?" we asked curiously. He opened several passports from European countries and showed us that a permanent place of residence was indicated in all of them, while our passports did not contain such data. "In our country nobody cares where one lives," we answered laughingly. "That is wrong!" declared the clerk, still holding our passports in his hand, as though deciding what to do with us. "All right, we will inform our government about it," we said jokingly.

"This is not a document, this is not an I.D.," the clerk continued stubbornly, ignoring our joke. He still continued to remain in a state of indecision, even when we took our key and started going up to our room.

In the elevator we immediately discussed the conflict that had just taken place: The clerk presented himself to us as a person willing to take risks, allowing people with improper documents into the hotel on his own responsibility. His action was to do us a great favor. We saw him as a person putting on a performance. We had absolutely no doubt that he had seen American passports many times. Our action was to play up to him, to join in his game.

It should be noted that when we checked out three days later, the clerk made an attempt to cheat us out of one hundred dollars!

3. The True Friend

Many times when remembering a real-life situation, we become vexed because we had acted a certain way and not another. In such cases we often think, "The next time that such a situation arises, I will definitely act in a different manner; I will reply differently." In other words, if a similar conflict repeats itself, I will make use of a different action.

A friend of mine once complained to me that one of our mutual acquaintances, let's call her Mrs. G, whenever answering the phone, would always say after an initial enthusiastic exchange of greetings, that she must break off the conversation because "someone is at the door." Lately it had been her husband every time. My friend could not believe in such frequent coincidence, but there was nothing else for her to do except say good-bye and hang up. At the same time, whenever Mrs. G herself calls our friend, no one ever appears "at the door."

Seeing that my friend was dissatisfied with her own behavior, I suggested to her that the next time Mrs. G's husband was "at the door" to call him to the phone to say "hello." In other words, I advised her to change her action.

Let us now analyze the conflict between Mrs. G and our friend. The leading side is naturally Mrs. G. Her main given circumstance is that the phone call interrupts her in doing something that is important to her, but out of politeness she cannot say it outright. The side of the conflict that Mrs. G presents each time to our friend is that she holds her in great affection, that she nurtures the warmest feelings towards her. Her action consists of extricating herself from the situation while preserving the appearance of friendship.

Our friend, meanwhile, sees Mrs. G as a self-centered person who always puts her own interests first. She does only what is convenient and necessary for her. Our friend's action was to avoid superfluous explanations — the situation was already quite clear to her. However, since she was dissatisfied with such a course of action, I advised her to change it to another, specifically to make fun of Mrs. G, to place her in an embarrassing situation, to teach her a lesson.

Training in the Workshop Environment

All of the above-mentioned real-life stories and situations for exercises can be performed in the form of improvisations with partners in a workshop environment.

We also recommend creating improvisations based on literary material. Within this context the actor should attempt to employ the literary material and situations which would allow him to depart from his customary or "normal" logic of thinking. In creating improvisations, you should not strive toward an exact reproduction of the circumstances found in the literary source. It is only important that the literary material you have chosen fires your imagination toward the creation of a story.

Fairy tales, fables, and short stories are especially suitable as a basis for improvisations. The material of a play is too complex, as a rule, for creating improvisations, since relations between the characters of a play are in a state of continuous development and depend on a multitude of circumstances. Besides, it is difficult to reveal the conflict that exists in an isolated scene taken out of the body of a play. It is necessary to study the entire play as a whole, for very often the conflict of a given scene is based on information supplied by the author in other parts of the play and through the words of the other characters not participating in the scene under consideration.

Write the story down in the form of a finished scene with a

beginning and an end of its own. This story should contain circumstances, characters, their interrelations and behavior. Try to avoid complex psychological circumstances, which usually necessitate lengthy descriptions.

Then you proceed to the conflict and determine the actions of the characters. Afterwards the participants are asked to play this scene in the form of an improvisation — this means that the dialog must be created spontaneously. The actor should get into the habit of using the text not as a goal in itself, but as a means for performing the action, as one of the adjustments. Otherwise the performers will drown in a pool of words, and as a result, they will lose the thread of the actions in which they are engaged.

We often construct improvisations based on literary material that describes people and situations from a different and unknown era, land, or culture. However, we should never attempt to reproduce the characters, situations, or ethnography of the material that has inspired us. Our attention should always be focused on the creation of conflicts and actions.

Following below are six improvisations based on different literary material. In all of the improvisations we have defined the conflicts, the actions, and the directions for the flow of energy. For purposes of illustration, two of them include the possible dialog for performing the actions.

The first two improvisations are inspired by fairy tales by the Italian writer Gianni Rodari which we read many years ago.

1. The Land of Roses

Once upon a time, a certain boy-wanderer found himself in a beautiful land of roses, where even the houses and pickets were woven of roses. Unable to resist the temptation, the boy plucked a rose. Suddenly, as though from under the ground, there arose before him a round-faced and charming policeman. He smilingly told the boy that plucking roses is forbidden in this land and that he must bear punishment for it, that is: He must either slap the policeman in the face twice or leave the land. In response to the boy's amazement and indignation, he explained that whoever once slaps an innocent person will never again break the law.

No matter how hard the boy tried to force himself to slap the policeman, he only succeeded in stroking his face. "Well, then you must leave our land," said the policeman, and the boy tearfully left the beautiful land of roses forever.

We must now find the conflict and the actions in this scene. The conflict: the policeman presents himself as a strict enforcer of the wise laws of this land. The boy, on the other hand, sees him as an eccentric: First of all, the boy's misdemeanor isn't all that serious, everything here is strewn with roses, and secondly, how is it possible to hit an innocent person? Where is the logic of it?

The policeman's action is to punish the boy. The boy's action is to find a correct approach to the eccentric, to establish relations with him, to be diplomatic.

Following is a suggested way of playing this scene, using only those words which are necessary to the performance of the action.

POLICEMAN: *(Smiling)* Young man, you have broken the law. It is forbidden to pluck roses in our land.

BOY: I didn't know. Take it back, please.

POLICEMAN: No, no, keep the rose. And now, immediately slap me twice in the face.

BOY: I don't understand you.

POLICEMAN: You must bear punishment for breaking the law. Either you slap me twice or leave the land. Such is the wise law of our land.

BOY: No, why should I slap you? You are so nice, and you are totally innocent.

POLICEMAN: That's the point. Whoever hits an innocent person will remember it for the rest of his life and will never again break the law.

BOY: But I promise that I will not break any laws.

POLICEMAN: In that case, I will have to say good-bye to you.

BOY: Well ... all right, I will try. Here. *(Strokes his face.)*

POLICEMAN: No, no, that is not a slap.

BOY: *(Crying)* I can't do otherwise ...

POLICEMAN: *(Barely holding back his own tears)* Please leave the land.

The policeman works up his energy — he is sorry for the boy, but he must enforce the law. The boy's energy streams towards the policeman — the latter's demand is bizarre. However, he restrains it, since he must persuade and placate the policeman, to convince him of the law's incongruity.

2. The Library Mouse

Once upon a time, an old library mouse came to visit her grandnephews. The nephews listened with wonder and delight to her stories of her extraordinary life, of how every day she ate not only Dutch cheese and sausage, but also cats.

A cat who was dozing nearby after a hearty meal heard these stories and jumped out of his ambush. At the sight of him the young mice ran off in great fright and only the library mouse, who had never seen a live cat in her life, remained on the spot.

The old mouse did not whet the cat's appetite, but the cat decided to have some fun. Pinning the mouse down, the cat asked her whether she was the mouse who ate cats.

"Ah, Your Highness," the mouse said apologetically. "How would I dare? It is only the ones in pictures, in books!" "Does that mean you destroy picture books?" the cat asked sternly. "But, Your Highness, that is my job. I am a library mouse! I eat not only, pardon, Your Highness, cats, but also houses, people, and even elephants. Recently I ate both Americas, the North and the South." The cat suddenly became terribly bored. He yawned widely, and taking advantage of it, the mouse slipped into the mouse-hole.

The leading side in this conflict is the cat. He sees the mouse as a pest, a nuisance. His action is to frighten her, to have some fun. The mouse sees herself as someone who performs her duty honorably. After all, she is not just a common mouse, but a learned theoretician. Her action is to save her life for the benefit of science. She does it by ingratiating herself with the ignorant cat.

The cat works up his energy to scare the mouse as much as possible. When he becomes bored, his energy dissipates and the mouse is able to escape.

Although the mouse is indignant at the ignorant cat, who obviously doesn't understand with whom he is dealing, her great fright forces her to work up her energy and flatter the cat, addressing him as "Your Highness."

3. The Model
We have sought to make an improvisation on the subject of a short story by O. Henry, which we had once read. The essence of the story is about a young artist who unexpectedly meets a pretty girl in whom he immediately sees the ideal model for a picture he has long wanted to do.

The artist makes a date with the girl in order to persuade her to pose for his picture. But seeing and sensing that the girl likes him, and that she is expecting something entirely different from him, he doesn't know how to broach such a delicate subject.

The artist ardently talks about the picture he has conceived, in the center of which is just such a beauty as her. Seeing the girl's interest and attraction, he finally decides to ask her to be his model. The confused girl reacts with total dismay.

Their relations can be characterized in the following manner. The artist is the leading character in the conflict. He presents himself as a creative person who has met his ideal. The girl, however, sees him as a person who is head over heels in love, to the extent that he even sees her in the center of his picture. His action is to arouse, to draw the girl into his creative plans. Her action is to let him know that his feelings are mutual.

The artist restrains his streaming energy, so as not to uncover his intentions all at once and thus frighten the girl off. The girl, too, restrains her energy: She is embarrassed to show her feelings right away.

4. The Functionary (inspired by A. Chekhov's short story *Death of a Functionary*)

The story takes place during a theatre performance. A certain functionary accidentally sneezes and sees that an elderly gentleman, sitting in front of him, mutters something crossly and begins to wipe his bald head with a handkerchief. Upon closer examination, this gentleman turns out to be an important person and the head of the institution in which the functionary serves. The functionary, scared out of his wits, immediately leans over and apologizes.

During the intermission, the functionary comes over to the important person and once more begins apologizing. The functionary then becomes distraught over the fact that his superior accepted his apologies somewhat absent-mindedly and even waved him off.

Upon returning home, he tells his wife what has happened and they decided that he should visit the important person in his office, in order to apologize profusely.

The scene that we are examining takes place in the important person's office. Having waited his turn, the functionary enters the office, and reminding his superior about the misunderstanding at the theatre, repeats his apologies. The important person responds with an impatient wave of his hand, saying that he has long forgotten the incident, and asks the next visitor to come in.

The dismayed functionary, certain that the important person

does not want to talk to him because he is still offended, proceeds to assure the latter that he did not sneeze on purpose, and that he has come expressly to deflect any possible suspicions. The important person, barely restraining his anger and suspecting that he is being laughed at, asks the functionary to leave.

In total despair the functionary makes a final attempt to vindicate himself in the eyes of his superior, but only succeeds in drawing a burst of wrath and even screaming from the latter. Overcome with fright, the functionary faints.

The main given circumstance is that in response to the functionary's sincere apology, the important person behaves strangely and suspiciously. Apparently he is harboring a grudge against him.

The conflict is that the functionary presents himself as someone who is full of deference and the greatest respect towards the important person. His action is to remove any possibility of doubts and suspicions about him. But the important person sees him as a troublemaker. His action is to rid himself of the other's importunate pestering.

The functionary's energy flows freely at his superior. He is ready to turn himself inside out, just to convince his superior of his love and devotion. The important person tries unsuccessfully to restrain his energy, but it subsequently breaks loose and flows over the functionary.

FUNCTIONARY: This is concerning my having sneezed on you. I haven't slept the whole night. My wife and I talked it over and decided that I should come to apologize.

SUPERIOR: Oh, God, I have already forgotten about it! Next, please ...

FUNCTIONARY: You see, you don't even want to talk to me. You are apparently angry. But I...

SUPERIOR: *(Speaks with annoyance.)* Are you laughing at me?

FUNCTIONARY: How could I! I couldn't even dream of it! But I ...

SUPERIOR: *(Indignantly)* Come now! I haven't seen anything like this!

FUNCTIONARY: But I didn't do it deliberately.

SUPERIOR: Leave my office, I have no time for this.

FUNCTIONARY: Perhaps I should come tomorrow?

SUPERIOR: Go away! Don't set foot in here again!*(The functionary faints.)*

5. Torch Song (inspired by John Cheever's short story)

Jack had known Joan for thirty years. Time has not made Joan look old. Her voice has always been soft and serene, and she has always worn black.

Once Joan spoke of her former lovers, and Jack gathered that they all had gotten into trouble: Some of them became very sick and died, one had poisoned himself, one was missing in the Atlantic, and one burned in his house. The last time Jack met Joan, at a party in her apartment, he wondered which of the men belonged to her. He decided on an Englishman who kept coughing into a handkerchief, and he was right.

Years have passed, and Jack's life has turned for the worst. He lost his job, ran out of money, and moved to a cheap furnished room. Then he got sick, the fever keeps him drowsy most of the time. Jack is sure that none of his friends know where he is, and he is glad of this.

One morning, Joan knocks on his door, walks in, and sits in a chair beside his bed. As always, her dress is black, her voice is low and serene.

"Why did you come?" is his first question.

"Because we have been friends for many years."

Jack looks at Joan suspiciously and asks how is that coughing Englishman, whom he met at Joan's party. But Joan could not remember him. "He's dead, isn't he?" Jack said. He pushes her off the bed, gets up himself, and tells her to get out.

"Who are you that you can smell misfortune and death?" he shouts. "Does it make you young to watch the dying? But you came too early — I still have many years ahead of me. But when they are over, I'll call you, as an old friend, and give you the pleasure of watching the dying. But now get out!"

"You poor, sick darling," Joan says. "I'll come back tonight."

After she leaves, Jack begins to dress himself. He stuffs his things into a suitcase, empties the ashtray, and sweeps the floor with his shirt, so that there will be no trace of his life, of his body, when that personification of death comes there in the evening.

Let us examine the scene of Joan and Jack's meeting, which

contains one conflict and one action. Jack's given circumstance is that all of the people with whom Joan is close die. The ailing Jack sees her as a personification of death, who has come for him. His action is to get rid of Joan, remove her from his life. He continues his action even after she leaves.

Joan sees herself as his old friend. Jack is in a desperate situation, he is sick and needs help. Her action is to calm him, pacify him. She does not contradict the sick man, she pays no attention to his feverish raving.

Jack's energy streams at Joan freely. Joan is forced to restrain her rush of energy, in order to avoid arguments with the sick man.

Refining an Improvisation to the Point of a Finished Scene

Any improvisation that has been acted out in the workshop environment can be refined to the state of a finished scene. To achieve this, one must write down the dialog and polish the performance of the improvisation with the help of the elements of the actor's technique: attitude towards the object, emotional memory, energy. At the same time one can also select and note any interesting mise-en-scènes that have been spontaneously discovered by the actors. We will demonstrate this process by using as an example the two improvisations "The Land of Roses" and "The Functionary."

In performing the improvisation, particular attention should be paid to how the partners evaluate each other. The student must be taught to listen and to hear, to look and to see, to be aware of what his partner wants from him. In other words, he must actively monitor his partner's action. Simultaneously, the actor must prepare himself for counteraction, which he will perform with the help of words, facial expressions, body movements, and stage props.

1. "The Land of Roses" Improvisation

The Object

What kind of objects can there be in "The Land of Roses"? The boy has an object that has been assigned to him by the author, the rose that he has plucked. Does this object bear a psychological load or is it simply a tool for performing the action? Naturally the rose bears a psychological load — for the boy it is a precious object, a symbol of the land that he has come to love. Such an attitude can be shown in the way the boy plucks the rose, touches it, smells and looks at it.

And what kind of an object can be devised for the policeman?

For example, we can place in his hands a large book containing the wise laws of his land. Such an object also bears a psychological load, giving the policeman essential moral support in performing his "ruthless" mission. He can thus open the book at the appropriate page and read the wording of the law to the boy. This book gives the policeman the faith that he needs to exist within the given circumstances of this story.

Emotional Memory

For us the "Land of Roses" is associated with the beautiful Hawaiian islands. Our memory brings back walls of flowers that change color three times a day, pink skies, aquamarine sea, white sand — everything as in a fairy tale.

2. "The Functionary" Improvisation

The Object

The author does not assign any psychologically-loaded objects to any of the characters in this story. However, we can provide the characters with objects that will assist them in performing their actions. For example, the functionary can be carrying a handkerchief, which he constantly uses to wipe the sweat of fear from his face. The superior can have many small objects on his desk. In his irritation, for example, he can crumple a piece of paper or break a pencil.

Emotional Memory

As we have already said, in performing a role each person must draw only upon his own emotional memory, i.e., use only what he has personally felt and experienced. We can only share the associations which personally arose in us in connection with the story.

I remembered something that had happened to me many years ago in New York City. Coming out of the subway and turning the wrong direction, I found myself in a deserted area, where I was surrounded by a gang of armed juvenile delinquents. As soon as I saw them, I immediately thought that I had made an absolutely irreparable mistake. I put myself in the place of the unfortunate functionary, who was convinced that he had made an irreparable mistake, and I experienced the desperate state in which he felt himself.

My memory also prompted me with what the superior was feeling. The particular incident took place in a railroad station in Germany. One of our friends came up to a low-level official with a question, and in confusion, not knowing how to ask him in German, said the only German phrase he knew: "Sprechen Sie Deutch?" (Do you speak German?) The official's face puffed up with indignation, then became pink, then turned scarlet — I was fully under the impression that he would burst on the spot. These associations came to me in connection with the image of the superior. When playing this role, I remember how that official was literally bursting from inside, and this helps me create a truthful image.

Individual Exercises at Home

The technique of the following exercises is the creation of various given circumstances, the related conflict and action, and the execution of the latter. These exercises can be performed at home with an imaginary partner.

An attentive reader might wonder at the statement above, since throughout our entire book we have specifically stressed the fact that stage action can only exist within the framework of live interaction between partners. We have also pointed out repeatedly the danger of working with an "imaginary" partner, because having fantasized his reactions to our actions, we thus rid ourselves of the necessity of live interaction on-stage and may lose the ability to react spontaneously to all the nuances of a partner's behavior.

Nevertheless, in one special case individual exercises with an imaginary partner are quite possible. Such exercises are constructed according to the following plan:

1. One must fantasize a certain circumstance (or combination of circumstances) that compel the leading side to enter into a conflict.

2. The leading side's position in the conflict and his action are then determined.

3. The student performs the action physically. This means that the student employs the facial expressions and body movements, and also, if the action demands it, the words that are appropriate to the given direction of energy. The action is performed by the leading side with an imaginary partner; however, the position of the one who is being led in the conflict is not constructed and his reaction is not fantasized, since he hasn't yet entered into the conflict and has not yet become aware that the action is directed against him.

4. Afterwards, one adds new given circumstances and observes the subsequent changes in the conflict, the action, and its execution.

Let us examine an example of such an exercise:

You are hosting a musical soiree in your home and people have gathered to listen to a pianist whom you have expressly invited. Suddenly two of your friends begin talking to each other during the performance. You immediately enter into a conflict with them, in which you become the leading side. Your position in the conflict is that you see them as tactless people who do not know how to behave. Your energy flows freely towards your partners, while at the same time you perform the obvious action of bringing your friends to order.

This can be physically expressed by your waving your hand at them, or even whispering something to them, or simply trying to meet their eyes. In your imagination you can see your partners, you can see the picture we have just described. However, you do not build up the position of those being led in the conflict and you do not imagine their reaction, since they haven't yet entered into the conflict with you.

The next step in doing this exercise is to expand and add to the given circumstances. Let us add a new circumstance: Those who are chatting are not simply your friends, but respected elderly ladies (or your colleagues, etc.). Nevertheless, you are the hostess and you must ensure a proper environment for the pianist. Your conflict will not change, it will remain as before; likewise your action will not change. However, the direction of the energy during the performance of the action will be somewhat different: Your energy streams towards the people in order to bring them to order, but you will be restraining it, since you are embarrassed to reprimand them. Consequently, the physical performance of the action, i.e., your facial and body movements, will be different. For example, you can put your finger to your lips and smilingly gesture for them to be quiet.

Now let us consider another given circumstance: The pianist whom you have invited is playing poorly and the audience has become terribly bored. Your conflict with the guests who have started talking will remain the same, and so will the action. However, the direction of the energy during your performance of the action will change once more: You realize that the listeners are bored with the pianist's poor performance just as you are yourself, but elementary politeness forces you to create a proper environment for his playing. You will proceed to work up your energy and gesture to the people to stop talking.

You can do these exercises physically at home without a partner. You will thus train your imagination and become used to changing the direction of your energy depending on the actual combination of the given circumstances.

The addition of one or another given circumstance to the original situation can lead to a change not only in the direction of the energy, but also in the conflict and action themselves. For example: I am offended at a friend of mine, who, as I have been told, says bad things about me. And now she is walking toward me on the street. I see her as a hypocrite (this is my position in the conflict which I am imposing upon her) and I am working up my energy to turn my back on her, which is difficult for me to do since I have always been on the best of terms with her. This is how I perform my action — to define our relationship, to punish her.

Now let us add a new circumstance to the old one (the friend who speaks ill of me). I am tied to this friend at our place of work and I am largely subordinate to her. In this case, my conflict and my action will change: I impose upon her that we are still friends, that our relations haven't changed. Accordingly, I suppress my sense of injury, I work up my energy, and with a smile, I wave to her. In this manner, I perform my action — to smooth over our relations.

Let us now suppose that my friend has had a nervous breakdown and gone through a period of severe personal problems. My attitude towards her will then change: I see her as an unstable person, who has lost touch with reality and who sees everything and everybody in somber tones. My energy streams forth to tell her off, but I restrain it; I put my arm around my friend's shoulders and invite her to visit me. Thus I perform the same action as in the previous example (smoothing over our relations), but I am applying my energy in another direction.

The training described above helps develop the habit of working with given circumstances, encourages an understanding of how their selection affects conflicts, actions, and their performance. Such training ensures a requisite basis for future work on the play and the role.

In choosing material for the exercises, begin with an examination of the simplest relations in life, without overburdening the exercises with complex psychological situations that you often come across in literature and drama. Try to envision the circumstances that you have imagined in motion — this already makes you think emotionally and allows you to feel the action you are performing internally.

Epilogue
The Actor's Transformation

The ultimate goal of a dramatic actor is the embodiment on-stage of the character of a person who has been created in the imagination. To achieve this one must re-create or experience on-stage the other person's feelings, anxieties, strivings, desires, thoughts, and physical behaviors. To this end, one must possess imagination, the ability to believe in the created fantasy, the ability to believe in the surrounding world on-stage as though it were real. In other words, the actor must begin living the full human life of the character he is playing. Such an internal reconstruction is the beginning of what is called "transformation."

The transformation can seldom occur in a flash of inspiration, which would allow the actor to immediately encompass the character in all of its psychophysical aspects. Although some cases are known, they are extremely rare. More to the point, the actor must possess a systematic method of gradually moving away from himself and towards the character, into another human individual that has been stipulated by the author.

Such a method, discovered by Stanislavsky and refined by his followers, is presented in this book. Stanislavsky pointed out that the extreme complexity of another person's character which the actor must recreate within himself, can only be comprehended more easily, truly and deeply when the actor interprets and defines his hero's logical line of action. It is not how he looks, or how energetically or slowly he speaks, or how loudly he laughs, or how nice his gait is, but rather how he behaves and in what logical sequence he performs his actions. It is the logic of behavior, leading to one action or another, which differentiates people and provides the possibility of forming the most precise opinion of them.

Accordingly, the problem of transformation consists of two sides of an integral creative process: 1. Studying the play according to events, constructing a logic of behavior for the character within the given circumstances of the play; 2. A practical implementation by the actor of the logical line of the role, staying within the character's logic of behavior. In the words of Stanislavsky, at this stage the actor must "proceed away from himself towards the character." That is, he must use his own human qualities to create another logic of behavior that has been stipulated by the author. Both of these sides may be examined separately only to a certain degree, because while studying the play, the actor achieves an internal realization of the character, and during the embodiment of the role's stage actions, there arises the need for a more precise definition of the character's behavior.

If the actor correctly exists within the given circumstances of the role and performs actions uncharacteristic of himself, but characteristic of the personage, and makes them his own, then at a certain stage of growing into a role he undergoes a change in his way of thinking and in his attitude towards the surrounding world. If this does not occur, then not a single external characteristic (make-up, costume, gait, manner of speech, etc.) can help him create the stage character.

Paradoxical though it may be, the actor himself should think about the transformation least of all. He must engage himself in comprehending the given circumstances, the conditions in which the character lives, his relations with the people around him, and the individual characteristics of the person he is portraying. And if, after grasping all of the above, he becomes infected with the essence of the character he is seeking to portray and subordinates himself and all his thoughts and feelings of the subtleties and peculiarities of another person's behavior, then the miracle of that which is called transformation will take place.

Acknowledgments

We are grateful to Penguin Putnam Inc. for kind permission to use material from Graham Greene's short story *A Shocking Accident*.

Our particular thanks to Professor Jean-Norman Benedetti, who drew our attention to the problem of establishing standard and workable English equivalents of Stanislavsky's terms.

Many thanks also to Natalia Sheniloff, Cheryle Franceschi, and our son, Eugene, for their help in preparing this book for publication.

Notes

Chapter One

[1] Stanislavskii, vol. 1, p. 299.

[2] Ibid., pp. 299-300.

[3] Stanislavsky was very skeptical of how the system was represented by some of his followers. In a conversation in August 1934, he said:

> Disciples ... A man stays in our theatre for a short time, passes through one–two roles, and becomes ... a disciple. But what I taught him to, what he had learned — it is unknown. He teaches the system, but the system is a very dangerous thing.
>
> Once it happened to me such a case. One prominent American actress decided to learn the system in order to further develop herself. In America, the system is taught by the former actors of the Second Studio [of the Moscow Art Theatre], Boleslavsky and Ouspenskaya. Well, she studied with them, understood everything, but could not play anything anymore, could not play — and that's all!
>
> She rushed to search for me, came to Europe, to Nice, but I had already left for Paris. She went there and has found me. "What is to be done?" asked she. So, I had to work with her, because I felt, to some degree, responsibility for my "disciples." True, they explained to her everything except for one little thing: *For what* everything takes place on the stage. They failed to put into her head that *everything is for the sake of the superobjective.* Well, who would have thought it possible — it seems that the people are intelligent.
>
> (Quoted in Zon, pp. 463–64. Obviously Stanislavsky was referring to his meeting with Stella Adler.)

[4] Stanislavskii, vol. 4, p. 267.

[5] Ibid., p. 519.

[6] Ibid., p. 297.

[7] Ibid., pp. 299-300.

[8] Ibid., p. 342.

[9] Quoted in Toporkov, p. 166.

[10] Stanislavskii, vol. 3, p. 499.

[11] Ibid., p. 450.

[12] Quoted in Toporkov, p. 164.

[13] Quoted in Kovshov, p. 80.

[14] Quoted in Toporkov, pp. 131-132.

[15] Stanislavsky and his followers continued to call the new approach to the work on a role as "the method of physical actions." However, one should not confuse this approach with the initial version of the method of physical actions, which was used by Stanislavsky in 1929-35.

[16] Kedrov, p. 194.

[17] Ibid., p. 191.

[18] Quoted in Kovshov, p. 91.

[19] Kedrov, p. 21.

[20] Ibid., p. 209.

[21] Kovshov, p. 49.

[22] Kedrov, p. 153.

[23] Popov, p. 243. First appeared in the newspaper *Sovetskoe Iskusstvo* [Soviet Art], 24 October 1950.

[24] Kedrov, p. 115.

[25] Ibid., p. 70. First appeared in *Sovetskoe Iskusstvo*, 30 December 1950.

[26] *Sovietskoe Iskusstvo*, 10 February 1951.

[27] A typewritten copy of this book can now be found in the Library of Congress.

[28] Stanislavskii, vol. 4.

[29] Knebel', p. 115.

[30] The original name of the method, *deistvennyi analiz*, appeared only in the late 1950s; Stanislavsky and Kedrov never used it. This name can be rendered in English as "analysis by action" or "analysis in action." In Georgii Tovstonogov's *The Profession of the Stage Director*, published in Moscow, the name is translated as "the method of active analysis."

[31] Vinogradskaia, p. 562.

[32] Tovstonogov, *Besedy s kollegami*, p. 213.

[33] Ibid., pp. 76-77.

[34] Ibid., p. 242.
[35] Ibid., pp. 65-66.
[36] Tovstonogov, *Zerkalo stseny*, p. 245.
[37] Ibid., p. 243.
[38] Ibid., p. 248.

Chapter Two

[1] Stanislavskii, vol. 3, p. 48.
[2] Vinogradskaia, p. 311.
[3] Levin, pp. 22-23.

Chapter Three

[1] Quoted in Kristi, p. 65.
[2] Quoted in Zon, p.466.
[3] Michael Chekhov, *To the Actor*.

Chapter Four

[1] A more detailed description of the different types of conflicts, and related examples, are given in Levin.
[2] Stanislavskii, vol. 2, p. 336. See also *An Actor Prepares*, p. 272.

Chapter Five

[1] In the words of Uta Hagen: "Only when you are talking aloud when alone is it a monolog. Anything else is a dialog! Someone can talk back to you with a look, a snort, a yawn, by turning away, by smiling, by giving you a concentrated look of attention, etc."
[2] Vinogradskaia, p. 496.
[3] Translation by Constance Garnett.
[4] Translation by Constance Garnett.

Bibliography

Benedetti, Jean. *Stanislavski and the Actor*. New York: Routledge/ Theatre Arts Books, 1998.

Chekhov, Michael. *To the Actor: On the Technique of Acting*. New York: Harper & Row, 1963.

Hagen, Uta and Frankel, Haskel. *Respect for Acting*. New York: Macmillan Publishing Co., 1973.

Kedrov, Mikhail Nikolaevich. *Stat'i, rechi, besedy, zametki (Collected Articles, Speeches, Conversations, Notes)*. Moscow: VTO, 1978.

Knebel', Mariia Osipovna, *O deistvennom analize p'esy i roli (On the Active Analysis of the Play and the Role)*. 3rd ed. Moscow: Iskusstvo, 1982 (1st ed. 1958).

Kovshov, Nikolai Dmitrievich. *Uroki M. N. Kedrova (M. N. Kedrov's Lessons)*. Moscow: Iskusstvo, 1983.

Kristi, Georgii Vladimirovich. *Vospitanie aktera shkoly Stanislavskogo (Training of an Actor of the Stanislavsky's School)*. 2nd ed. Moscow: Iskusstvo, 1978.

Levin, Irina and Igor. *Working on the Play and the Role: Stanislavsky Method of Analysing the Characters in a Drama*. Chicago: Ivan R. Dee, 1992.

Okhitovich, L. A. *Metod fizicheskikh deistvii: Monografiia o poslednem otkrytii K. S. Stanislavskogo (Method of Physical Actions: A Monograph on the Final Discovery of K. S. Stanislavsky)*. Moscow: unpublished, 1948.

Popov, Aleksei Dmitrievich. *Tvorheskoe nasledie (Artistic Legacy)*, vol.2. Moscow: VTO, 1980.

Stanislavskii, Konstantin Sergeevich. *Sobranie sochinenii v vos'mi tomakh (Collected Works in Eight Volumes)*, vols. 1-4. Moscow: Iskusstvo, 1954-1961.

There are English translations of volumes 1 to 4:

Stanislavsky, Konstantin. *My Life in Art*. New York: Theatre Art Books, 1952.

-------. *An Actor Prepares*. New York: Theatre Art Books, 1967.

-------. *Building a Character.* New York: Routledge/Theatre Art Books, 1977.

-------. *Creating a Role.* New York: Theatre Art Books, 1961. The main shortcoming of the American editions of volumes 2–4 is that they leave out a majority of rough notes and drafts concerning the latter years of Stanislavsky's life.

Toporkov, Vasilii Osipovich. *K. S. Stanislavskii na repetitsii: Vospominaniia (K. S. Stanislavsky in Rehearsal: Memoirs).* Moscow: Iskusstvo, 1950.

Tovstonogov, Georgii Aleksandrovich. *Zerkalo stseny (The Mirror of the Stage),* vol. 1. Leningrad: Iskusstvo, 1984.

-------. *Besedy s kollegami: Popytka osmysleniia rezhisserskogo opyta (Conversations with Colleagues: An Attempt of Comprehension of the Director's Experience).* Moscow: STD RSFSR, 1988.

-------. *The Profession of the Stage-Director.* Moscow: Progress Publishers, 1972.

Vinogradskaia, I., ed. *Stanislavskii repetiruet: Zapisi i stenogrammy repetitsii (Stanislavsky Directs: Notes and Shorthand Records of Rehearsals).* Moscow: STD RSFSR, 1987.

Zon, B. V. *"Vstrechi s K. S. Stanislavskii (Meetings with K. S. Stanislavsky),"* *Teatral'noe nasledstvo: Materialy, pis'ma, issledovania (Theatre Legacy: Materials, Letters, Research),* eds. I. Grabar' et al., vol. 1. Moscow: Akademia Nauk SSSR, 1955.

Index

About the Authors

Irina Levin was born in St. Petersburg, Russia, where she worked for thirteen years as an actress in repertory theatres, performed solo dramatic reading concert programs, and worked as a drama teacher and director at a theatre-studio. Since her emigration to the United States in 1976, she has conducted an audition class in New York, taught acting courses at Catholic University, and directed a number of plays. Igor Levin is a mathematician. He holds a Ph.D. in computer science and is the author of numerous scientific papers. They are the authors of *Methodology of Working on the Play and the Role* (1990) and *Working on the Play and the Role* (1992).

Irina and Igor Levin live in Washington, DC.

Order Form

Meriwether Publishing Ltd.
PO Box 7710
Colorado Springs CO 80933-7710
Phone: 800-937-5297 Fax: 719-594-9916
Website: www.meriwether.com

Please send me the following books:

_____ **The Stanislavsky Secret #BK-B254**   **$16.95**
by Irina and Igor Levin
Not a system, not a method but a way of thinking

_____ **The Art of Acting #BK-B171**   **$16.95**
by Carlton Colyer
The complete artist-actor training process

_____ **Directing for the Stage #BK-B169**   **$19.95**
by Terry John Converse
A workshop guide of creative exercises and projects

_____ **Play Directing in the School #BK-B214**   **$17.95**
by David Grote
A drama director's survival guide

_____ **Everything About Theatre! #BK-B200**   **$19.95**
by Robert L. Lee
The guidebook of theatre fundamentals

_____ **Theatre Alive #BK-B178**   **$39.95**
by Dr. Norman A. Bert
An introductory anthology of world drama

_____ **The Theatre Audition Book #BK-B224**   **$16.95**
by Gerald Lee Ratliff
*Playing monologs from contemporary, modern,
period and classical plays*

These and other fine Meriwether Publishing books are available at
your local bookstore or direct from the publisher. Prices subject to
change without notice. Check our website or call for current prices.

Name: _____

Organization name: _____

Address: _____

City: _____ State: _____

Zip: _____ Phone: _____
❑ **Check enclosed**
❑ **Visa / MasterCard / Discover #** _____
                                                    Expiration
Signature: _____   *date:* _____
            (required for credit card orders)

Colorado residents: Please add 3% sales tax.
Shipping: Include $2.75 for the first book and 50¢ for each additional book ordered.

❑ *Please send me a copy of your complete catalog of books and plays.*